Countertransference and the Therapist's Inner Experience

Perils and Possibilities

Countertransference and the Therapist's Inner Experience

Perils and Possibilities

Charles J. Gelso
University of Maryland
Jeffrey A. Hayes
The Pennsylvania State University

LEA LAWRENCE ERLBAUM ASSOCIATES, PUBLISHERS
2007 Mahwah, New Jersey London

Lawrence Erlbaum Associates, Inc., Publishers
10 Industrial Avenue
Mahwah, New Jersey 07430
www.erlbaum.com

Cover design by Tomai Maridou

Library of Congress Cataloging-in-Publication Data

Countertransference and the therapist's inner experience : perils and possibilities / Charles J. Gelso and Jeffrey A. Hayes.

p. cm.

Includes bibliographical references and index.

ISBN 978-0-8058-4696-6 — 0-8058-4696-4 (cloth : alk. paper)

ISBN 978-0-8058-6082-5 — 0-8058-6082-7 (pbk. : alk. paper)

ISBN 978-1-4106-1622-7 — 1-4106-1622-3 (e book)

1. Countertransference (Psychology) 2. Psychotherapist and patient. I. Hayes, Jeffrey A. (Jeffrey Alan) II. Title.

[DNLM: 1. Countertransference (Psychology) WM 62 G321c 2007]

RC489.C89C6822 2007

616.89'17—dc22

2006021276
CIP

Books published by Lawrence Erlbaum Associates are printed on acid-free paper, and their bindings are chosen for strength and durability.

Printed in the United States of America

10 9 8 7 6 5 4 3 2 1

Contents

Preface

This book is about the inner world of the psychotherapist, and how that world comes into play and is enacted within the psychotherapy relationship. This inner world (variously labeled *subjectivity* and *experiential world*) is a vital part of the therapeutic relationship that develops between psychotherapist and patient, a relationship that has been repeatedly shown to be a major part of whether psychotherapy works or not, how it works, and how well it works with a given patient and patients in general. Within the therapeutic relationship, the construct to which our greatest attention is devoted in this book is called *countertransference*.

Since Freud first discussed countertransference in the early part of the 20th century, the concept has had a complex life, to say the least. Initially eschewed as something that was bad and needed to be done away with, the broader field of psychotherapy maintained an ambivalent attitude toward countertransference for many years. Even now, as there is much greater acceptance of countertransference, we tend to keep it at a safe distance, often conceptualizing it as an experience created by the patient, as not having to do with the therapist's unresolved conflicts and vulnerabilities, and as something that occurs in our trainees or perhaps in we more experienced therapists in our distant pasts. In fact, it is our contention that countertransference centrally implicates the therapist and his or her unresolved conflicts and vulnerabilities, and that it occurs in virtually all psychotherapies. This is so because, by virtue of our humanity, we therapists all possess sore spots—unresolved inner conflicts and vulnerabilities that the very personal work of psychotherapy is bound to touch upon and expose.

In chapter 1, we explore in detail the history and current status of countertransference in psychotherapy and psychoanalysis. Then in chapter 2 we present our integrative theory of countertransference. This conception is connected to the major current definitions of countertransference, but also different from them. As part of our conception, we seek to clarify what countertransference is *not*, as well as what it is. In chapter 3 we discuss the operation of countertransference across the three predominant theory clusters in psychotherapy: psychoanalytic and/or psychodynamic, humanistic and/or experiential, and cognitive and/or behavioral. As we make clear in these chapters, although countertransference as a theoretical concept originated within psychoanalysis, countertransference occurs in all psychotherapies and in all psychotherapists. Throughout this book, we focus on countertransference as a universal, and we seek to show its relevance across theories.

A key thesis in this book is that when countertransference is not managed well, it exerts numerous adverse effects. However, when appropriately managed, countertransference has the potential to greatly benefit the treatment. Chapter 5 is devoted to how the negative effects of countertransference can be prevented or minimized, and how countertransference can be used in this positive sense. Here we present our conception of the five factors involved in the management of countertransference and, in turn, of how countertransference facilitates progress in psychotherapy.

Although countertransference is the key concept of this book, the book is not all about countertransference. There is a major portion of the therapist's subjectivity that is not countertransference, and in chapter 4 we explore this noncountertransferential aspect of the therapist's subjectivity. In this portion of subjectivity reside all of the therapist's feelings, thoughts, images, and visceral sensations that are essentially conflict free—that do not result from some conflict or vulnerability in the therapist. This aspect of subjectivity possesses great potential for benefit, for it includes inner processes such as empathy, liking, caring, and even forms of loving. These states generally are deeply beneficial parts of psychotherapy. Some of them, such as empathy, have a long history in psychotherapy theory and research, and their benefits are widely recognized. Other states, such as noneroticized love, have generally been avoided, perhaps because of our tendency to view strong affect wrongly as reflecting countertransference problems, along with the tendency to equate wrongly loving feelings with sexuality.

After decades of neglect, the past 20 years have witnessed an upsurge in empirical research on countertransference. In chapter 6 we seek to provide a synthesis of this research, keeping in mind our aim of speaking to the practicing psychotherapist as well as the empirical researcher. We focus especially on findings that have been supported by more than one study and on those that seem most clinically relevant. As you will see, a corpus of clinically meaningful findings has developed over the years, and yet much more is needed. The topic of countertransference is a very clinically rich one, but it is also, stated simply, a bear to study! Our hope is that this chapter, and the book more generally, will foster an increased interest in the empirical study of countertransference.

In our final chapter, we attempt to provide the reader with some take-home messages, so to speak. Frankly, our fear in writing this chapter was that the reader would skip the rest of the book and go to the take-home messages. On the other hand, it seemed equally risky that, having read the previous chapters, the reader might skip the last chapter altogether. In the end, we felt it was worth the risk, because concluding statements and recommendations can be tremendously useful to readers. Our hope is that, if you read chapter 7 first, it whets your appetite to dig deeper and read the rest of the story!

We have each worked on the topic of countertransference and the therapist's experiential world for many years. I, Charlie, began my work on the topic in the early 1980s and Jeff joined me in the late 1980s, first as my graduate student, and subsequently as collaborator. In our work on countertransference and the therapist's subjectivity, we have taken the roles of teacher, clinical supervisor, empirical researcher, theoretician, and psychotherapist. Our experience in all of these roles has been intellectually challenging, which has been what we wanted; and it has been deeply rewarding. We have combined our theoretical predilections toward psychoanalysis and humanism in an effort to develop an integrative conception of countertransference, one that cuts across diverse perspectives. The fact that we have these differing orientations has helped each of us refrain from parochialism and allowed each to enrich the thinking of the other. We leave it to the reader to be the judge of whether we have succeeded in this effort to speak to readers from diverse perspectives.

ACKNOWLEDGMENTS

We wish to thank several people for their assistance during the process of writing this book. Our editor at Lawrence Erlbaum Associates, Susan Milmoe, deserves our appreciation for her interest in our topic and for shepherding our proposal through the initial stages with the publishing house. Similarly, we have appreciated Steve Rutter's encouragement and his suggestions about how to improve our manuscript. Elizabeth Doschek has graciously offered helpful comments on chapters. Chris Andrus gave willingly of her time to prepare references. Finally, we are grateful to the many patients with whom we have worked over the years who have endured our countertransference reactions and taught us much.

—Charles J. Gelso and Jeffrey A. Hayes

1

The Past and the Present: The Evolution of Countertransference

Countertransference has had a long, complex, and unsteady history in the field of psychotherapy. Originating within the confines of Freudian thought, it was paid scant attention for many decades, even within psychoanalysis. However, over the past 25 years or so, interest in the construct has greatly increased and widened. Psychoanalytic therapists have become vitally interested in countertransference. But others have also become interested, as we discuss. Over the years, the meaning of countertransference, too, has evolved, such that at the current time, there exists some shared understandings and some fundamental disagreements about just what countertransference is and what its role is in both psychodynamically based treatments and nondynamic therapies.

It is our contention that countertransference is a part of all psychotherapy. Anytime there is a relationship between a therapist and a client or patient, there will be varying degrees and kinds of countertransference. Although the psychoanalytic practitioner may typically pay closest attention to countertransference, the behavior therapist, experiential therapist, and every other kind of therapist surely experiences countertransference. It is no less important for these therapists, in comparison to the analytic therapist, to manage their countertransference reactions effectively. Furthermore, as we discuss in this book (especially chap. 4), we believe countertransference is best understood within the broader context of what is referred to as the therapist's *subjectivity*—the affective experience that is an ongoing part of each and every therapy hour.

In chapter 1, we discuss how conceptions of countertransference originated in Freud's thinking. We examine how conceptions of this construct have developed over the nearly 100 years since it was first written about, and we offer a critique of current conceptions. Finally, we examine points of agreement and contention in current thought.

Historically, the literature on countertransference has been rooted in psychoanalysis; therefore, much of what we examine in this chapter will stem from that literature. However, because it is our contention that countertransference is universal and is an important part of all therapies, we also seek to relate our discussion to nonanalytic approaches.

FREUD'S LEGACY: AMBIVALENCE

As is the case with so many phenomena in psychotherapy, in order to gain an in-depth understanding of the topic of this book, it is helpful, if not necessary, to begin with some observations of the originator of the "talking cure." Although Sigmund Freud did not have a lot to say specifically about countertransference, he did offer some observations that may well have set the stage for and formed the foundation of current thought about this complex construct. In certain ways, Freud's suggestions about countertransference and the analyst's attention to his or her feelings and unconscious seemed contradictory. These contradictions left the field of psychotherapy with an ambivalent attitude toward countertransference, an ambivalence that has pervaded our history and seems present even today.

Freud urged therapists to study themselves and their own reactions to patients, to penetrate their own unconscious minds, in order to deeply understand the inner workings of their patients. For example, when discussing the basic ground rules of psychoanalytic therapy, Freud focused on the analyst/therapist's awareness of his or her own unconscious:

> All these rules which I have brought forward coincide at one point which is easily discernible. They all aim at creating for the physician a complement to the "fundamental rule of psycho-analysis" for the patient. Just as the patient must relate all that self-observation can detect, and must restrain all the logical and affective objections which would urge him to select, so the physician must put himself in a position to use all that is told him for the purpose of interpretation and recognition of what is hidden in the unconscious, without sub-

> stituting a censorship of his own for the selection which the patient forgoes. Expressed in a formula, *he must bend his own unconscious like a receptive organ towards the emerging unconscious of the patient, be as the receiver of the telephone to the disc. As the receiver transmutes the electric vibrations induced by the sound-waves back again into sound-waves, so is the physician's unconscious mind able to reconstruct the patient's unconscious, which has directed his associations, for the communications derived from it.* (Freud, 1912/1959b, p. 328, italics added)

Although this statement is naturally geared toward psychoanalysis, it is easily applied to all of psychotherapy. Thus, therapists need to study and understand themselves deeply and use this understanding in order to understand their patients deeply.

During the same time period, Freud made another statement that was directly related to countertransference and moved the field in a different direction. As part of a discussion of innovations in psychoanalysis, he indicated:

> We have begun to consider the "counter-transference," which arises in the physician as a result of the patient's influence on his [the physician's] unconscious feelings, and have nearly come to the point of requiring the physician to recognize and over come this counter-transference in himself. Now that a larger number of people have come to practice psycho-analysis and mutually exchange their experiences, we have noticed that every analyst's achievement is limited by what his own complexes and resistances permit, and consequently we require that he should begin his practice with a self-analysis and should extend and deepen this constantly while making his observations of his patients. Anyone who cannot succeed in this self-analysis may without more ado regard himself as unable to treat neurotics by analysis. (Freud, 1910/1959, p. 289)

In this statement, Freud makes clear his view that countertransference is injurious to treatment and to the patient. When he says that the therapist must perform a self-analysis and "extend and deepen this constantly," he implies that this is an ongoing process. However, the therapist must come to grips with and resolve his or her own complexes and resistances. If the therapist cannot succeed in this self-analysis, he or she should not be a therapist. In this quote, it is implied that nothing of worth can come from countertransference.

Furthermore, in his famous Surgeon's Quote, Freud (1912/1959b) tells us, "I cannot recommend my colleagues emphatically enough to take as a model in psycho-analytic treatment the surgeon who puts aside all his own feelings, including that of human sympathy, and concentrates his mind on one single purpose, that of performing the operation as skillfully as possible" (p. 327). So it appears that not only must analysts eliminate their countertransference, but they should also put aside all of their feelings in order to do effective work.

When the three quotes just presented are examined together, we see a clear basis for the ambivalent attitude toward countertransference that seemed evident over many decades. On one hand, we as therapists are to understand our unconscious and use this understanding in every treatment. On the other hand, we are to put aside all of our feelings and eliminate countertransference. Epstein and Feiner (1988) capture this mixed attitude when they tell us that these two themes, countertransference as a hindrance and the therapist's use of his or her own unconscious to understand the patient, "have been intertwined, like a double helix, throughout the historical development of psychoanalytic conceptions of countertransference" (p. 282), and of treatment itself.

As we have noted, countertransference had been understudied for many decades following Freud's statements. Why was this so? Many have viewed this neglect as a function of the pejorative view of countertransference held by Freud. If no good can come from a phenomenon, and if the therapist who does not succeed in getting rid of it should give up his or her vocation, then that phenomenon needs to be avoided. And it was avoided, in both the clinical literature and the empirical research literature. In more recent times, however, definitions and conceptions of countertransference have shifted, and a key part of this shift has been the view that countertransference can be an aid to treatment as well as a hindrance. Furthermore, current thinking suggests that countertransference cannot ever be completely done away with. The therapist cannot eliminate countertransference by having the kind of personal psychotherapy that would allow him or her to work through all major "soft spots," such that countertransference would never appear. Instead, no matter what the definition of countertransference, and no matter how well "therapized" the therapist, there is general agreement that countertransference will be a part of his or her work in therapy.

Epstein and Feiner (1988) indicate that at least three different conceptions of countertransference are can be seen in the psychoanalytic literature. We now describe these conceptions, along with a fourth one, and note how each may or may not relate to nonanalytic therapies.

CONCEPTIONS OF COUNTERTRANSFERENCE

The Classical View

The classical conception of countertransference was originated by Freud (1910/1959) and was stated most forcefully many years ago by Annie

Reich (1951, 1960). Countertransference is conceptualized as the therapist's largely unconscious, conflict-based reactions to the patient's transference. In this sense, countertransference may be seen as the therapist's transference to the patient's transference. Epstein and Feiner (1988) note that countertransference in the classical conception contains both neurotic and nonneurotic elements. However, it is the neurotic elements that make it most undesirable. As we have elsewhere discussed (Gelso & Hayes, 2002), unresolved conflicts originating in the therapist's early childhood are triggered by the patient's transference, and may be manifested in any of a number of ways. The countertransference may take many shapes and forms. It may cloud the therapist's understanding, thus creating confusion in the therapist's attempt to grasp the patient's issues. It may also create distortions in the therapist of the patient's psyche and self. For the behavior therapist, for example, countertransference may make it more difficult for the therapist to delineate the specific behaviors that need to be changed, the reinforcement history that has caused those behaviors, and the interventions needed to change them. Finally, countertransference may cause the therapist to behave with the patient in any of a wide range of antitherapeutic ways. A case vignette from clinical supervision done by the first author may help to exemplify countertransference from the classical definition:

> The therapist was a 26-year-old woman in the second year of her doctoral program in Counseling Psychology. She was seeing the client as part of her third therapy practicum. All indications were that she was an excellent developing therapist. She had been seeing the client, a 20-year-old college junior, in weekly therapy for approximately 5 months.
>
> The client came from a background in which her father was an alcoholic who paid little attention to her needs. The mother was deeply mistrusting and, while supportive of the client in many ways, communicated in myriad ways that her daughter could not rely on others and must struggle to be independent of them. In relationships, including her family, the client usually took a "parentified" role, while at the same time, as her therapist noted, "seemed terrified of being hurt by anyone and is extremely guarded and protective of herself." Outwardly, the client created an impression of being "businesslike and successful."
>
> The client brought her protective shell with her to therapy, and found it difficult to trust her therapist or allow herself to be vulnerable with or in front of the therapist. However, she did work extremely hard in therapy, as she did in virtually all aspects of her life. In the transference, the client appeared to experience the therapist as the good mother who could protect

> her and provide her answers, but also as the dangerous mother—the dangerous, untrustworthy internalized object that the client's own mother disowned and projected onto others. As for the countertransference that got stirred by this transference, it may be best to present the therapist's own words: "Complicating the matter is my countertransference, which involves the need to please and/or take care of people, and to take actions, to DO SOMETHING, in order to help. This plays itself out in several ways: First, the client asks a lot of questions and is often concerned about the success the therapy will have, and I feel the need to appease her rather than to be curious about her questions or take them up as therapy material; second, I often feel helpless or miserable with her because my 'doing' is seemingly fruitless, when in reality she is a very nice person, and a good client who is working very hard.
>
> Further complicating the transference/countertransference is that my issues are very similar to the client's. Since I have not resolved my own issues, this causes me more negative feelings, such as fear that I will not be able to help the client because I myself do not know what to do. We also play off each other, and are both very task-oriented, so she asks me what to do and I feel the need to answer; each of us is concerned about pleasing the other and what the other might think. I struggle to fight these feelings and to simply relax, as I also try to understand and help my client."

As may be seen in the vignette presented, the client's transference hooked into the therapist's unresolved issues, and created a transference reaction in the therapist toward the client. What made the therapist's reactions transferential? These reactions reflected still unresolved conflicts emanating from the therapist's childhood. The therapist's conflictual responses mirrored how this therapist responded within and to her own family. We should note that much of the therapist's reactions were under conscious control, or at least partially understood. This is unlike most countertransference from the classical perspective. The therapist's awareness of her countertransference was enhanced because she was in weekly supervision, in which her internal and external reactions were explored in terms of their relation to the client's issues, transference and otherwise.

Countertransference from the classical perspective is not seen as benefiting the work of therapy. Rather, as indicated, it is a hindrance that needs to be eliminated through the therapist's resolution of his or her problems and conflicts, and it is every therapist's task to overcome the vulnerabilities that cause countertransference.

Although it is certainly true that therapists exhibit transference reactions to their patients' transferences, and it is further true and important that therapists must continually seek to resolve their own issues as they may emerge in and color their work with patients, the classical view is often seen as too narrow a conception of countertransference (Epstein & Feiner, 1979; Gelso & Hayes, 1998, 2002). Thus, it is scientifically and clinically helpful to also view as countertransference those reactions in the therapist that are not transferential, and it is equally useful to view the triggers of countertransference as client material that is not necessarily transferential. Moreover, however conflictual in the therapist, it is helpful to consider the possible benefits that may result from countertransference and what needs to occur in the therapist for those benefits to accrue.

The Totalistic View

The classical position held sway for many decades. However, as the scope of psychoanalysis widened, and as the kinds of patient pathologies being treated by analysts and analytic therapists broadened, another view of countertransference emerged. The totalistic conception of countertransference emerged in the 1950s and was further developed in subsequent years (Heimann, 1950; Kernberg, 1965; Little, 1951). It was in part a reaction to the perceived narrowness of the classical position, as well as a result of the widening scope of psychoanalysis.

In the totalistic conception, all of the therapist's attitudes and feelings toward the patient are viewed as countertransference (Epstein & Feiner, 1988). All reactions are important, all should be studied, and all may be usefully placed under the very broad heading of countertransference. This position served to legitimize countertransference and make it something to be analyzed, understood, and used in the therapy, rather than avoided. Thus, as the totalistic position gained ascendancy within psychoanalysis, countertransference came to be seen as something that could greatly benefit the work, provided that the therapist studied his or her internal and external reactions and used these to further understanding of the patient, the patient's impact on others, and hidden parts of the patient's internal world. One's internal reactions are important for a variety of reasons. For one, they likely will mirror how others in the patient's life react to the patient. Secondly, the therapist's experience of the client is a superior means of beginning to grasp the client's transference. In other words, what the therapist feels at a given moment may well reveal what the patient is pulling for or is experiencing within the transference. For example, if the therapist feels sharply protective of the patient, the transference may involve the patient's unconscious projection onto the therapist of the mother or father who failed to protect or care sufficiently for the patient. In this sense, the patient is unconsciously showing the therapist how the patient was treated as a child and how the patient felt about that.

Third, the therapist's feelings may reveal aspects of the patient's internal world that are not otherwise apparent. For example, the therapist's feeling tired in sessions may be a response to hidden depression, inner tiredness, or emotional avoidance in the patient, which may not be revealed to the therapist through the patient's verbalizations. For all of these reasons and more, the therapist's internal experience of the patient may be tremendously important in understanding and responding to the patient.

It is significant that the totalistic position gained popularity as psychoanalytic therapists began doing more work with severely disturbed patients. Those with borderline and narcissistic pathology, in particular, often evoke intense and perhaps inevitable reactions in their therapists. For example, much has been written about hate and rage in the therapist when working with patients suffering from borderline personality disorders (see early papers by Winnicott, 1949, and the extensive writings of Kernberg, 1975, 1976). Such reactions seem so natural a response to the intense negative reactions of the patient, reactions that are so often disowned and projected onto the therapist, that they appear to be both (a) a counter to the patient's transference and (b) not based on unresolved conflicts within the therapist. In other words, these striking reactions in the therapist seemed like a normal and regular part of treatment with borderline patients, and yet seemed also like they ought to be placed under the countertransference umbrella. This view is nicely captured by Kernberg (1965) when he states:

> When dealing with borderline or severely regressed patients, as contrasted to those presenting symptomatic neurosis and many character disorders, the therapist tends to experience, rather soon in treatment, intensive emotional reactions having more to do with the patient's premature, intense and chaotic transference and with the therapist's capacity to withstand psychological stress and anxiety, than with any specific problem of the therapist's past. Thus, countertransference becomes an important diagnostic tool, giving information of the degree of regression in the patient, his predominant emotional position vis-à-vis the therapist, and the changes occurring in this position. The more intense and premature the therapist's emotional reactions to the patient, the more threatening it becomes to the therapist's neutrality, the more it has a quickly changing, fluctuating, and chaotic nature—the more we can think the therapist is in the presence of severe regression in the patient. (p. 54)

The totalistic perspective has many advantages, not the least of which is to make the therapist's emotional experience a highly significant and vital part of psychoanalytic work. The totalistic position in a certain way normalizes these feelings and makes them less threatening to admit openly and to study. (We focus on the value of such a position in psychoanalysis rather than, for example, the humanistic and/or experiential therapies because in the latter, the therapist's emotional experience was always viewed as a vital part of the therapeutic enterprise.) However, the fact that severely regressed patients evoke intense reactions in their therapists, and that all of the therapist's emotional reactions are important, is not a reason to view all of the therapist's reactions as countertransferential. In fact, as we have elsewhere stated (Gelso & Hayes, 1998), if all emotional reactions are viewed as countertransference, then there would be no need at all for the term. We could just refer to these reactions as emotional reactions. Furthermore, if all emotional reactions were to be viewed as countertransference, a need undoubtedly would emerge among clinicians and researchers to divide this global concept into those rooted in the therapist's unresolved conflicts or "soft spots," and those that are a normal, healthy, expectable reaction to the patient's material. This is in fact what has occurred among some investigators. For example, Kiesler (1996, 2001), a leading interpersonal theorist, differentiates countertransference reactions into subjective and objective types, paralleling the distinctions we have just made. A question worth pondering is whether so-called objective countertransferences (which are viewed as normal, healthy, and expectable) should be seen as countertransferential at all, rather than simply the therapist's emotional reactions. Our conclusion is that it is best to reserve the term countertransference to Kiesler's subjective type. If the term is to be optimally useful to scientists and practitioners, we believe it must be differentiated from emotional reactions that are not defined as countertransference. To know a thing means in part to know what it is not. Thus, in a word, the totalistic perspective is so broad as to be of limited value scientifically and probably clinically.

The Complementary View

The third conception of countertransference noted by Epstein and Feiner (1988) is called the *complementary view*. Countertransference is conceptualized as a complement or counterpart to the patient's transference or style of relating. The complementary view shares with the totalistic view the belief that therapists' reactions (at least internal ones) are often inevitable, given the patient's defenses and ways of relating. The distinctiveness of this complementary conception resides in its articulation of the psychological dance that is often carried out between therapist and patient. Each constantly affects and influences both internal and external reactions in the other, and this circle continues throughout the treatment. Patients consciously or unconsciously "pull" for certain reactions from their therapists, and therapists experience the impulse to respond to their patients' pulls in particular ways, which in turn creates reactions in patients, and so forth. Many years ago, this position was powerfully articulated by Heinrich Racker (1957, 1968), and is seen today especially in the work of interpersonal theorists (e.g., Butler, Flasher, & Strupp, 1993; Kiesler, 1996, 2001; Levenson, 1995).

The complementary view is interestingly captured by what Racker (1957, 1968) terms the "law of tallion." This law states that every positive transference is met with a positive countertransference, and every negative transference is met with a negative countertransference. For Racker and others espousing the complementary view, countertransference reactions, at least internal ones, are inevitable. At the same time, one should not assume that this means that such reactions are psychologically healthy. For example, Racker examines what he terms *countertransference neurosis*, which is often tied to unresolved issues in the therapist, while being precipitated by the patient's transference neurosis. To Racker, such a countertransference neurosis is inevitable and is often dominated by the therapist's psychopathology. At the same time, if the therapist understands that such reactions are precipitated by the patient's transference, these therapist reactions may be understood and used to gain important information about the patient's underlying issues.

Within the object relations school of psychoanalysis, a particular defense mechanism is often thought of as being the trigger for complementary countertransference (Feldman, 1997; Klein, 1955/1975; Ogden, 1982, 1994). This defense, projective identification, results from the patient's unconsciously disowning or splitting off certain affects or parts of the self and projecting them into the therapist. The therapist unconsciously internalizes these affects and experiences the impulse to act them out, for example, to be the hyperaggressive object that is projected into him or her. In any event, the well-functioning therapist is able usually to refrain from acting out *lex talionis* ("an eye for an eye, a tooth for a tooth"), even though it is a "normal" reaction to act it out. Instead, the good therapist controls the eye-for-an-eye impulse, and seeks to understand what in the patient is creating this internal state. As Epstein and Feiner (1988) exemplify:

> Once the analyst has identified his own emotional state, he is able to consider the questions "Why have I fallen into this position now?", "What has

> this to do with the analytic process?", "What internal self and object relations might the patient be enacting with me?", "Do my feelings indicate that he needs my love, or that he wants to triumph over me?", "Is the patient from the position of his child-self relating to me as if I were his superego?", and "Do my feelings indicate the he wants me to punish or criticize or demean him?" (p. 288)

Although much of the work stemming from the complementary position is heavily psychoanalytic, it can be readily translated into less arcane language, as well as concepts that are nonanalytic. Terms used by Kiesler (1996, 2001), for example, such as patient "pulls" on the therapist, easily relate to any theoretical position. One need not resort to constructs such as the primitive defense mechanisms, or even unconscious processes, to grasp that the patient and therapist mutually influence one another in a way that creates certain internal reactions in the therapist, which he or she then understands or acts out.

Although the complementary or counterpart conception captures the interpersonal aspect of countertransference better than other conceptions (Gelso, 2004), it too has limitations. The conceptualization of countertransference as pulls on the therapist originating in the patient's transference, nontransference material, or style of relating does not take into account enough the therapist and his or her internal world as a causal factor. Thus, even though it is acknowledged that the therapist's issues are certainly implicated, the focus seems too much on the patient's defenses and/or pathology as the cause. This is most clearly seen in much of the writing about projective identification, in which it seems that the patient's denied affects are almost magically put into the therapist without sufficient attention to the issues within the therapist that allow for these affects to penetrate him or her, and more importantly, impel him or her to act them out (see Eagle, 2000, for a thoughtful exploration of this phenomenon). As one of us (Gelso, 2004) noted, the complementary view "tends to ignore what the therapist brings to the table and how the therapist, along with the patient, co-creates relationship dynamics" (p. 234).

The Relational View

A perspective that overlaps considerably with the complementary view and that more likely gets at the therapist's contribution to the deeply interactive nature of countertransference is termed the *relational perspective* (Gelso, 2004). This perspective does not posit an inevitability of certain therapist reactions to the patient's overt and covert material, as does the complementary view. Originating from object relations theory more broadly, the relational perspective is often referred to as a two-person psychology, in contrast to the more classical psychoanalytic theories, which are often seen as representing a one-person psychology. At the core, classical theories seem to view much of the therapy process as originating from the patient's defenses, conflicts, and, more broadly, personality. And the effective therapist acts as an empathic but neutral observer, one who stays outside of the patient's conflicts and provides well-timed and accurate interpretations. The relational theorists, however, emphasize co-construction; that is, whatever happens in the hour is jointly constructed by therapist and patient. Both shape the nature of transference and both shape the nature of countertransference, as well. Countertransference then is a product of the inevitable interaction of the patient's dynamics (his or her transference, realistic expression, personality, etc.) and the therapist's dynamics (unresolved conflicts, personality, needs, realistic expression, etc.).

One limitation of the relational perspective is the flip side of its very strength (Gelso, 2004). In its emphasis on co-construction, the reality that each participant in the therapy relationship brings his or her own set of issues, defenses, and dynamics to the table may not be fully appreciated. Furthermore, as one reads the very persuasive and influential work of leading relational therapists such as Aron (1996) and Mitchell (1988, 1997), what seems to get lost is the fact that each participant will behave in similar ways across relationships and that there is a core of each human being that dictates this (see Eagle, 2003). People who do not have this core, in fact, and who change in a chameleonlike fashion to meet the demands of every situation and relationship, are usually seen as deficient in one way or another. Many see this as a core element of narcissistic pathology (e.g., Kohut, 1984). Of course, human beings also differ from situation to situation, but if the core element that makes us the same across relationships is ignored or underappreciated, the therapy relationship and outcome will suffer for it.

THE PAST AND THE PRESENT

As we have noted, thinking about countertransference originated with Sigmund Freud. Although he had little to say about it, what he did say about countertransference had an enormous impact, for better and for worse. His classical view held sway for several decades. To be sure, there were some important contributions by others in the early decades of the 20th century. Ferenzi and Rank (1923) were among the first to delve into this topic. In focusing on the ways in which countertransference may affect the transference and thus the work of analysis, they stated:

> The narcissism of the analyst seems suited to create a particularly fruitful source of mistakes; among others the development of a kind of narcissistic countertransference which provokes the person being analyzed into pushing into the foreground certain things which flatter the analyst and, on the other hand, into suppressing remarks and associations of an unpleasant nature in relation to him. (p. 41)

Other key contributors in the early years were Stern (1923), Glover (1927), W. Reich (1933), Fenichel (1940), and Horney (1939). Horney's comments are particularly important because they focus on the analyst's issues that seem to be other than displacement and transference. She states:

> The principle that the analyst's emotional reactions should be understood as a "countertransference" may be objected to on the same grounds as the concept of transference. According to this principle, when an analyst reacts with inner irritation to a patient's tendency to defeat his efforts, he many be identifying the patient with his own father, and thus repeating an infantile situation in which he felt defeated by the father. If, however, the analyst's emotional reactions are understood in the light of his own character structure as it is affected by the patient's actual behavior, it will be seen that his irritation may have arisen because he has, for example, the fantastic notion that he must be able to cure every case and hence feels it a personal humiliation if he does not succeed. (p. 166)

Horney is telling us that it may be the analyst's character structure as affected by the patient's behavior rather than displacement from the analyst's own father that is the countertransference. So we see that there were certain debates in those early years. Some writers focused on countertransference as a reaction to transference (similar to the complementary and also somewhat to the totalistic views), whereas others focused on the analyst's transference (Orr, 1954). Most authors addressed the unresolved issues of the analyst, whether they be manifested as displacements from early objects, personality factors, or current unresolved conflicts.

The general view was that countertransference needed to be resolved if the work was to be effective. During these years, countertransference was still in the clinical and theoretical closet. It was not something that was readily spoken about, since it was so connected with the analyst's psychopathology, and because of the prevalent view that such pathology could and should be resolved with the proper training and personal analysis. However, as the second half of the 20th century emerged, so too did markedly different views of countertransference. The totalist and complementary positions were spearheaded by thinkers such as Winnicott (1949), Fromm-Reichmann (1950), Heimann (1950), Little (1951, 1957), Cohen (1952), and Tauber (1954). Countertransference for this group of analysts was more likely to be seen as potentially useful, inevitable, and not rooted in the analyst's unresolved conflicts or character.

Outside of the sphere of psychoanalysis, a number of therapists have discussed countertransference in recent years. For example, Norcross (2001), a leading integrative therapist, tells us "... All theoretical traditions, moreover, recognize the therapist's contribution to the treatment process and the need for therapist self-care when experiencing the looming despair, sudden rage, or boundary confusion that is all part of countertransference" (p. 981). Our search for material on countertransference leads us to conclude that few behavior and cognitive-behavior therapists addressed this construct in their writing, although some address what they consider unhelpful behaviors that may have their origins in the therapist's unresolved issues. For example, in presenting her cognitive-behavior therapy for the treatment of borderline personality disorder, Marsha Linehan (1993) discusses what she calls "therapy-interfering behaviors of the therapist" (p. 138–141). These include a range of behaviors often thought of as rooted in countertransference (e.g., insecurity about one's skills; anger, hostility, and frustration directed at the patient; "blaming the patient" attitudes), although some of them simply seem to point to lack of clinical ability. Linehan notes that these therapy-interfering behaviors are what analytic therapists usually refer to as countertransference. Albert Ellis (2001) more directly addresses countertransference from his position as the originator of rational-emotive behavior therapy. Florence Kaslow (2001) does likewise for couples and family therapy, while also noting the great dearth of attention to countertransference in that area, with the exception of the family therapists who are explicitly psychoanalytic. We have more to say in chapter 3 about countertransference in the nonanalytic therapies.

Using Countertransference to Benefit the Work

How was countertransference to be used in a way that allowed it to aid the treatment? Epstein and Feiner (1988) detail four of what they call "working orientations" to the use of countertransference. Although Epstein and Feiner focus on psychoanalysis and analytic therapy, these working orientations may be readily applied to other theoretical approaches. In the first working orientation, countertransference is attended to when difficulties arise in the therapist. These difficulties may take the form of emotional disturbances, disturbances in attention or concentration, and in actual behavior, such as under- or overresponding to the patient. When interferences such as these occur, the therapist reflects inwardly for the source of the problem. This orientation most closely fits the classical view of countertransference. However, it is also the most common usage of cognitive and cognitive-behavioral therapists, who only attend to countertransference when they experience emotional conflict with their patients, and in particular when they find themselves behaving in ways that do not fit their treatment aims.

A second working orientation involves the therapist's self-examination of inner emotional conflicts as a means of gaining an understanding of the patient's contribution. The idea here is that the therapist's conflicts are stirred by the patient's dynamics, so understanding these conflicts will shed light on the patient's issues in a way that would not be readily possible otherwise. A third working orientation involves using the totality of the therapist's emotional experience to understand the patient in the here and now. Those who espouse the totalist position within psychoanalysis have this working orientation. In addition, the humanistic and/or experiential therapist pays close attention to his or her inner experiencing in the here and now, whether or not something is amiss inwardly. Such inner experience communicates to the therapist much about what it is like to be in a relationship with the patient.

The final working orientation involves the view that countertransference inevitably infiltrates the patient's unconscious process, and that such infiltrations need to be constantly monitored by the therapist through studying the patient's associations and other responses. It is unclear, however, just how the infiltration by countertransference of the patient's unconscious is used to benefit the work, above and beyond the therapist's self-examination.

WHERE ARE WE NOW? POINTS OF CONVERGENCE AND CONTENTION

Despite the great complexity of the term countertransference, and the many and divergent views of it, there is actually considerable agreement currently about what it is and how it is best dealt with (Gabbard, 2001; Kiesler, 2001). Let us take a look as these points of convergence.

Shared Views of Countertransference

First, as Gabbard (2001) points out, psychoanalytic theorists from diverse perspectives (e.g., ego psychology, object relations theory) share the view that, at least to some extent, countertransference is always a joint creation of the therapist and the patient. Theories differ in just how much of countertransference is due to the patient and the therapist, but Gabbard (2001) comments, "there is a remarkable degree of agreement that what the patient projects onto the clinician and what the clinician brings to the situation are both relevant to the end result of countertransference" (p. 989). The same patient will evoke different reactions in different therapists, and the same therapist will respond differently to different patients. Both therapist and patient are part of the countertransference, although, as we discuss in chapter 2, it is important to appreciate the roots of countertransference as residing in the therapist, and his or her personality, anxiety, and defenses.

A second point of agreement noted by Gabbard (2001) is that the patient will inevitably attempt to transform the therapist into a transference object. Further, the therapist must then work hard to pull him or herself out of this role or transference–countertransference cycle into which the patient pushes him or her. Gabbard naturally conceptualizes this second point from the perspective of psychoanalysis. One need not do so, however, for the point to be made. From a nonanalytic perspective, one can conceptualize all humans as aiming to create certain reactions in others toward them, and this tendency may be seen as intensified in intimate relationships. In the intimate relationship called psychotherapy, patients exhibit certain pulls on their therapists. These originate in the patients' needs and anxieties. Some of these pulls are unhealthy for the patient and reflect his or her pathology. Analytic theorists have used terms like *projective identification*, *role responsiveness*, and *countertransference enactment* to get at these pulls and what the analyst does with and in response to them.

To the extent that the pulls represent the patient's defenses, or the patient's maladaptive ways of dealing with others, the therapist must resist enacting what is being pulled for. If this is all that was required, therapy and countertransference might be very easy to work with. However, as Gabbard (2001) astutely points out, if the therapist simply resists the pull with many patients, more difficulties may arise. For example, in working with patients suffering from borderline personality disorder, the therapist is often placed into the role of the bad object, for example, the parent who formed an abusive relationship with the patient during the patient's childhood. As part of this dynamic, the patient behaves contemptuously toward the therapist. If the therapist simply resists being placed into the role of the bad object, and remains unaffected, the patient is likely to escalate and become more contemptuous toward the therapist. The relationship then becomes poisoned by these interpersonal dynamics. However, if the therapist allows him or herself to be placed in that role, and responds angrily and abusively, the relationship is also poisoned. Instead the therapist must take a middle ground, by perhaps experiencing some anger, but maintaining his or her capacity for empathy and for helping the patient understand the dynamics that are operating.

Gabbard provides a case example to demonstrate this middle ground. He describes work with Rachel, a 28-year-old woman diagnosed with borderline personality disorder. Rachel began one session by plopping herself down in her chair, burying her face in her hands, and being silent. In response to Gabbard's inquiry about what was going on with her, Rachel snapped, "What does it look like? If I wanted to talk I would! You're always probing around for something." The therapist responded that he was concerned about her, given her suicidal thoughts recently, and that he wanted to find out how she was doing. Rachel then accused him of only being concerned about being sued. The therapist became irritated and replied, "That's simply not fair or accurate. I worry about you and care about your safety." Rachel responded, "What do you mean? You wouldn't even see me if my parents weren't paying you." Gabbard (2001) then shares his subsequent thinking and responding as follows:

> I was silent for a few minutes, realizing that I had once again been provoked into becoming irritated, a familiar pattern in our 3 months of therapy. I silently noted that she had recreated the same kind of angry but impotent feelings in me that she had so often provoked in her parents. I reflected a moment and then said to her, "Rachel, I feel like we've entered familiar territory here. You seem to resent my efforts and make accusations against me. I get irritated and defensive and make things worse. Then we reach a stalemate where I feel frustrated and impotent and you feel you're not getting any help. How do you understand this pattern, and what do you think we can do about it" (p. 987)

In working with such patients, this cycle will get repeated over and over, and progress is very gradual. The key point here is that this therapist was able to attain the middle ground that is needed in dealing with tremendously frustrating and often very painful affects that are created by the patient. In chapter 2, we have more to say about which aspects of such therapist reactions are aptly considered countertransference and which are better viewed as simply the therapist's affective experience and reactions, albeit extremely important reactions for the success of the treatment.

A third area of agreement articulated by Gabbard (2001) is that the therapist or analyst is not and cannot be a "blank screen" who maintains total neutrality and anonymity. In fact, it is almost unthinkable that this could ever have been the case, even as some traditional analysts strived for it. Scrutiny of cases presented by Freud and the early analysts attests to this. These were very real people responding to their patients in deeply human and personal ways. Given this reality, the therapist's task is far more complex than it would be if the therapist could indeed be a blank screen. The therapist must pay close attention to his or her inner workings, while at the same time respond with some degree of spontaneity and a full degree of humanness. J. R. Greenberg (1991) noted how this kind and degree of responsiveness in the therapist serves to expose him or her to the patient's conscious and unconscious scrutiny and how self-protectiveness is a defense against fear of such exposure.

In addition to the three points of agreement that we have been discussing, let us note others. Here we draw heavily from Kiesler (2001), and we follow each point with some commentary.

1. *When countertransference is occurring, mental contents are not mystically transported from patient to therapist; rather, it is the patient's behavior during the session that evokes or pulls reciprocal therapist experiences.* When reading some psychoanalytic treatises about patient defenses, such as projective identification, one has the impression that there is something almost magical about the effect the patient has on the therapist, as if the patient were magically transporting affects into the therapist. Instead, what stirs the therapist's behavior is often very subtle behavior on the part of the patient. Such patient behavior may be nonverbal and it may be masked from direct observation, for example, passive aggressiveness. The reader is referred to a thoughtful critique by Eagle (2000) of the therapist serving as a magical repository of patient affects. Eagle is critical of many theorists who take a complementary view of countertransference (e.g., Racker, 1968) because they seem to imply that the therapist inevitably takes in, identifies with, and mirrors the patient's affects.

2. *The real issue is not whether the therapist experiences or shows emotion with clients, but whether the therapist's emotions are harmful or useful.* As Brown (2001) tells us, "Therapy is, in fact, about the heart. It's a work of emotion" (p. 1012). Psychotherapy is an affective experience. As we listen to our patient's painful stories and participate with them in their own experiencing, it is natural that we experience affect. In fact, the absence of emotion in the therapist is more likely due to countertransference-based conflicts than is the existence of emotion. At the same time, not all emotion is helpful and at times acting on emotion will be unhelpful or harmful. Whether the therapist's emotion is harmful or helpful depends on many factors, among them (a) the nature of the emotion, (b) the intensity of emotion, (c) the extent to which the emotion reflects the therapist's unresolved conflicts or prob-

lems, and (d) whether the emotion reflects an acting out of what is being pulled by the patient (e.g., the patient's transference).

3. *The therapist's disclosure of his or her countertransference-based feelings and thoughts may at times be highly useful in helping the patient confront and change his or her maladaptive interpersonal behavior.* Although virtually all theoretical positions would agree with this statement as it stands, there are wide differences of opinion on just how much to disclose and, indeed, what to disclose. For interpersonalists such as Kiesler (1996, 2001), the good therapist shares with the patient in a nonjudgmental way the effect the client's affect and behavior are having on the therapist. Such feedback for the interpersonalist may be extremely helpful in showing the patient in the immediacy of the therapeutic relationship how the patient affects others, including the therapist, and how others feel about that. Feedback also helps the patient consider more deeply than he or she had what is going on inside (e.g., fears, wishes, defenses) that causes these behaviors toward others.

To therapists of other dynamic persuasions, disclosures of personal feelings depend on what is perceived as helpful for a given patient, as well as how the feedback will be taken in and used by the patient. When the feedback is negative, pointing to a problematic behavior in the patient, it is our experience that most often the patients who seem to need it most (those with the most problematic behaviors) will have the fewest resources to use negative feedback effectively and wisely. Be that as it may, psychodynamic therapists other than the interpersonalists are much more wary about disclosing what they feel in response to patient pulls.

Probably theorists of all persuasions agree that therapists need to have a sense of where they are coming from before disclosing their feelings to their patients. When countertransference is of the kind that originates in the therapist's unresolved conflicts and problems, probably all approaches to therapy would advocate restraint in sharing these reactions with the patient.

4. *Countertransference may be experienced internally and/or expressed externally, and in this sense, countertransference is part of the therapist's phenomenology as well as being part of the therapist's overt actions.* As Kiesler (2001, p. 1058) notes, countertransference "noticeably affects the therapist's cognitions, feelings, attributions, memories, and fantasies, as well as the therapist's verbal and nonverbal actions" (p. 1058). He further comments that when countertransference is operating, internal events become "hot" and rigid, and verbal and nonverbal behavior becomes intense and rigid. At the same time, as is discussed in subsequent chapters, it is possible for the therapist to understand in the moment his or her "hot buttons" and not act them out with the patient. Indeed, we would offer that the best therapists are adept at this process of quickly getting a sense of

whether their reactions are being significantly colored or intensified by their own issues. In other words, even if the gifted therapist does not know in the moment what those issues are, he or she is able to get a sense that something is awry, for example, that he or she is feeling something due to some sore spot being rubbed on, at least enough to not act these issues out on the client. Researches of our team several years ago uncovered that those therapists perceived by their peers as being excellent were seen as having more of this kind of self-insight (Van Wagoner, Gelso, Hayes, & Diemer, 1991).

This is not to say that the outstanding therapist never enacts countertransference-based behavior and always comes to grips with conflicts that are being aroused before they come out in action. We would maintain that all outstanding therapists get caught from time to time acting out countertransference-based behavior. It is just that the best therapists are better able to control the most egregious behaviors (e.g., hostile and/or destructive behavior, seductive behavior) and excel at catching themselves before the relationship or the patient has been injured by countertransference-based behaviors. From a psychoanalytic perspective, Gabbard (2001) tells us:

> Writings on technique suggest a much greater tolerance for the inevitable partial enactments of countertransference that occur in a treatment process. These enactments provide valuable information about what is being recreated in the psychotherapeutic or psychoanalytic setting. In this regard, therapists must recognize that they will be drawn into various roles in the course of the therapy and that maintaining an artificial aloofness is neither desirable nor helpful. (p. 990)

Points of Contention in the Current Scene

As is evident, there are many points of agreement about countertransference. However, there are also some substantial differences among the different theories and even within theories. The most fundamental difference pertains to the extent to which countertransference is a manifestation of the therapist's unresolved conflicts. Some believe that for the concept to make any sense, it must involve the therapist's needs, conflicts, or "soft spots." The therapist's issues, in other words, are seen as the origin of countertransference, even as the patient's behaviors may be seen as triggers. Other therapists take a more totalistic or complementary position, believing that countertransference is any therapist affect, and that it can be an "average expectable" reaction on the part of the therapist to a given pull from the patient. In this sense, it may not be based on a therapist's unresolved conflict at all, but rather be the precise reaction that would be expected from what the patient is doing. For this group of theorists, countertransference must be divided into types, as we have discussed earlier: One type that is based on conflict and a second type that represents the average expectable reaction on the part of a therapist to a given patient's behavioral expression.

One might actually represent the aforementioned disagreement as a continuum, with the two viewpoints residing on opposite ends. Therapists may fall at any point on this continuum. Although we are offering our own theoretical conception in the next chapters, the element of this current debate that is most troublesome to us is reflected in our observation that all too few therapists are aware of which of these two positions they are advocating when discussing countertransference. In fact, we have often observed the definition of countertransference shifting from one position to another within the same communication. One example of the manifestation of this confusion is that therapist or writer who seems to define countertransference in the broadest terms (the totalistic position) and then comments on how problematic therapist behaviors are a result of the countertransference, as if the countertransference were being imbued with a special meaning beyond, simply put, the therapist's feelings. In other words, one here is simply saying that the therapist's feelings are causing this or that reaction, but by calling the cause the countertransference, it is as if that cause were much more or different from simply the therapist's feelings.

Beyond this definitional point of contention, there are many disagreements that are best seen as matters of degree and not kind. As we have noted, how and when countertransference reactions should be revealed to the patient has been a major source of contention for over half a century. Most agree that some countertransference reactions may be helpfully shared with the patient in some ways, but beyond this point, there is much disagreement as to which reactions and in what ways.

A final significant disagreement pertains to whether the fundamental source of the countertransference within the therapist needs to be dealt with. Some theorists, especially those with a more behavioral emphasis, would not view it as necessary to examine the roots of a countertransference reaction in the therapist. They would more likely focus on the therapy-impeding behaviors and the need to modify these if therapy is to be successful. The more analytic therapist would argue that the underlying cause is important because it will affect how the particular reaction is expressed by the therapist and how the other behaviors that go along with it are also expressed. For example, the therapist getting drowsy with his gay patient, tied to the therapist's homophobia and fears of his own sexuality, may mean something dramatically different for the therapy than the therapist getting drowsy because of his chronic sleep deprivation due to an infant in the household.

CONCLUSION

The construct, countertransference, has come a long way since Freud first coined the term nearly a century ago. It has come out of the psychoanalytic closet and is now seen as a vital element of psychoanalytic treatment, one that has the power to damage the treatment and the patient, as well as to allow for a deeper emotional and intellectual understanding of the patient than would be otherwise possible. Although there are different conceptions of countertransference, there are also broad areas of agreement. Key among them is the view that countertransference involves both the participants in the psychotherapy drama, even though it is the therapist's contribution that countertransference is and must be most concerned with. The key disagreement revolves around the extent to which countertransference is rooted in unresolved conflicts and issues within the therapist or includes therapist's emotional responses that are "natural reactions" to what the patient is pulling for.

Outside of psychoanalytic and, more broadly, psychodynamic theories, countertransference is not often discussed in depth, despite the fact that it is one of the closest things to a universal phenomenon that exists in psychotherapy. In chapter 3, we explore countertransference and, more generally, the therapist's emotional reactions to the patient as these occur in nonanalytic therapies.

What has been missing in the clinical literature for many years is a cohesive theory of countertransference, its definition, its source, and how it is to be used in the interest of the therapy and the patient. In chapter 2, we present our theory of countertransference, based on more than two decades of research and theoretical development. Subsequent chapters are devoted to a theory of factors involved in managing countertransference so that it is beneficial to the therapeutic process.

2

An Integrative Conception of Countertransference

In this chapter, we present a conception of countertransference that originates from both clinical practice and our research spanning more than two decades. This conception contains elements of each of the four viewpoints presented in chapter 1: the classical, totalistic, complementary, and relational views. At the same time, our conception differs from each of these perspectives. Like the classical view, we believe that countertransference is best seen as rooted in the therapist and his or her inner conflicts and vulnerabilities. However, unlike the classical position, we do not see countertransference as inevitably pernicious, and we also see it in broader terms. For example, countertransference is not just the therapist's transference to the patient's transference, but instead includes the therapist's nontransference reactions to the patient's nontransference material.

Our position also shares the totalist's belief that all therapist reactions are important and that countertransference may benefit the work if used wisely by the therapist, although we clearly do not share the totalist's view that all of the therapist's emotional reactions to the patient ought to be classified under the broad countertransference umbrella. As for the complementary position, we agree that the therapist's countertransference is often a reaction to the patient's material and, further, that patients unconsciously seek to elicit certain affects and thoughts from their therapists. This aim on the part of the patient exerts of powerful pull on the therapist. However, we do not agree with the complementarist's belief that (a) therapist' reactions are inevitable or nearly so, (b) that countertransference has little to do with the dynamics and unresolved issues of the therapist, or indeed (c) that the therapist's affects mirror the patient's internal world because the therapist identifies with people who populate that internal world (e.g., Racker, 1968). Finally, we share the relational therapist's belief that all aspects of the therapeutic relationship, including countertransference, are jointly constructed by the therapist and patient. We differ from the relational position in that our focus is more on the therapist as the fundamental agent of countertransference, and in this sense, the therapist is more central to the process than the patient.

Although the concept of *countertransference*, and the term itself, originate in psychoanalytic thought and practice, our attempt has been to frame a theory that would be applicable to practice from any theoretical perspective. As we discuss, inasmuch as therapists' emotional issues and conflicts come into play in therapies of all orientations and durations, countertransference is surely one of the universal concepts in psychotherapy. Furthermore, the therapist's ability to be aware of countertransference, manage it, and use it for the sake of the work is one of his or her most potent tools. To the extent that the therapist's self-awareness is poor, countertransference has the power to damage the treatment process and relationship irreparably.

What might be the ingredients of a clinically and scientifically meaningful theory of countertransference? These ingredients are not too different from the ingredients of any good scientific and clinical theory (see Gelso, 2006). First and foremost, a key ingredient is a definition that differentiates countertransference phenomena from the therapist's reactions that are other than countertransference. All too often the literature and clinical discussions of countertransference seem to use the term as a shorthand for all of the therapist's emotionally based reactions, without acknowledgment and at times seemingly without awareness that this totalist viewpoint is being used. And yet, even when countertransference appears to be used as shorthand for the therapist's emotions or subjectivity, there appears to be some unspoken implication that it is more, perhaps much more. It is not uncommon for authors to take a totalistic position, thus viewing all emotionally based therapist reactions as countertransference, and then refer to the countertransference as the cause of events in therapy, as if the countertransference were more than or deeper than simply the therapist's feelings toward the patient.

We seek to go beyond the totalistic conception of countertransference and delimit the construct, showing what it is and what it is not. Although such delimitation is a necessary ingredient of any good scientific theory, a useful theory must not be too narrow or parochial. Because countertransference is seen as a universal in psychotherapy, a sound conception of it should transcend theoretical lines. That is, the construct is not owned by any particular theory, and it should be theorized about in a way that demonstrates its applicability to treatment of any theoretical orientation. Similarly, a good theory should be comprehensive. In the case of countertransference, such a theory should address key elements of the construct: (a) where it originates; (b) its triggers or precipitants; (c) how it becomes manifested; (d) what therapists need to do or be in order to control, manage, or utilize it; and (e) what its effects are on the process and outcomes of treatment. Subsequently, we present considerations on each of these elements, or what we refer to as the *structure of countertransference*.

A meaningful theory of countertransference ought to be useful in practice and it should be scientifically generative. Regarding practice, such a theory should help guide therapists' thinking about and understanding of their countertransference and other emotional reactions to their patients, and it should help them figure out what to do with these reactions. Finally, by *scientific generativity*, we refer to the vaunted heuristic function of a theory—to its ability to stimulate further research and theory. In order to do so, such a theory needs to be stated with sufficient precision, specificity, and clarity. In presenting our conception now, we have been mindful of the ingredients of a good theory, and have sought to adhere to them. The reader will of course be the final arbiter of how much we have succeeded in this effort.

DEFINING COUNTERTRANSFERENCE: WHAT IT IS AND WHAT IT IS NOT

Countertransference may be usefully defined as the therapist's internal or external reactions that are shaped by the therapist's past or present emotional conflicts and vulnerabilities. Several aspects of this definition require clarification. First, we note that our definition of countertransference is rooted in the therapist's emotional conflicts or vulnerabilities. Although the therapeutic relationship and its elements (e.g., countertransference, transference, working alliance) are always co-created by patient and therapist, and although patient behaviors and characteristics certainly stimulate countertransference, if a therapist reaction is to be considered countertransferential, it must centrally implicate some unresolved issue or vulnerability in the therapist. At the same time, there usually is a trigger for countertransference that resides outside the therapist. That trigger is most often some subtle or overt behavior on the part of the patient. In other words, the patient says or does something (or more likely an array of things) that connects to an area of unresolved conflict or vulnerability in the therapist. The trigger, however, may also be the therapeutic situation or frame, for example, the help-giving situation. As the trigger moves away from specific patient behaviors and toward the general frame of therapy, the kind of countertransference being exhibited is more likely to be chronic. (In text to come, we discuss the distinction between chronic and acute countertransference.)

A second aspect of the definition that should be clarified is that this definition refers to the past or present conflicts and vulnerabilities. The conflict may reflect historical experiences, experiences in early childhood that have been sealed away from consciousness. These historical experiences may be only rarely activated in the therapist's life, but the memory of them may get stirred up by some aspect of the patient's related experience and exhibited behavior. When such therapist conflicts are touched upon, the reaction may resemble transference in the sense that he or she may react to the patient as if the patient represented figures from the therapist's past. More likely than such transference, however, are the therapist's internal reactions that seem a little off center and/or behaviors that don't hit the mark in terms of what the patient needs. For example:

> The patient is a 40-year-old political scientist who has been in dynamically based therapy for 2 years, once a week. Mary is hardworking and has made significant progress, but is plagued by feelings that she never gets enough, stemming from a childhood in which both her parents loved her but seemed devoid of empathy. Her only way to get their sympathetic attention was to be physically ill or to fall apart emotionally. Naturally, this sense of not getting enough, of at times emotionally starving, is transported into Mary's therapy. Despite a good working alliance, during a period of the work, her complaints that the therapist (a seasoned 52-year-old analytically oriented therapist) was not providing enough support stirred up very old feelings in the therapist of failing to be what people wanted him to be, of being a disappointment. This sense of failing created anxiety that the therapist unconsciously sought

to allay through angry feelings and wishes to tell the patient just how competent he was and what good therapy she was getting.

Although one might make a case that the therapist's reaction represents transference, and that his perceptions of the patient were distortions that represented early, frustrating figures in his own life, such a formulation contains too much excess baggage. It is more to the point to view the therapist's emotional reaction as stemming from old wounds or vulnerabilities that have gotten activated by the patient's material.

On the other hand, the conflicts and vulnerabilities may be in the present. The therapist who has experienced a painful loss in his or her recent life, for example, may have a conflicted reaction to material the patient presents related to loss. The therapist may withdraw from the patient's pain, respond with excessive support, change the topic, or react to his or her own painful feelings in any of a number of ways. Of course, the present vulnerability may be painfully heightened if the therapist has a history of unresolved losses. In this sense, if a current trauma occurs in a therapist who has a history of related trauma, the vulnerability to patient material in the area of the trauma is greatly magnified.

We have been discussing past or present conflicts and vulnerabilities as part of the definition of countertransference. Another aspect of the definition requiring amplification is that countertransference involves *internal* or *external reactions* on the part of the therapist. Internal reactions include feelings, emotions, thoughts, or bodily sensations. External reactions include verbal and nonverbal behavior toward to patient. Generally speaking, internal reactions are important to be aware of. Indeed, a key aspect of using the countertransference in the service of the work is becoming aware of what one is feeling and thinking toward the patient during the therapy hour, and even outside of the hour. The importance of being aware of one's internal countertransference reactions has been supported in research demonstrating that such awareness is an important part of the therapist's empathic understanding of the patient, as well as the therapist's being responsive to the feelings the patient is expressing rather than avoiding those feelings (Peabody & Gelso, 1982; Robbins & Jolkovski, 1987; Latts & Gelso, 1995).

To be aware of one's feelings, or even to "bend his own unconscious like a receptive organ towards the transmitting unconscious of the patient," as Freud (1912/1959b, p. 328) advocated, is not too daunting a task for most therapists. Remember, people who choose to become therapists, and who receive extensive training in self-awareness, are usually good at being aware of their feelings. They enjoy such awareness. However, the process of becoming aware is much more difficult, much thornier, when that awareness pertains to unresolved conflict and vulnerabilities, whether rooted in the past or in the present. One does not automatically and easily become aware when usually hidden conflicts and vulnerabilities are at the root of the reactions. The road to understanding likely begins with a sense in the therapist that something is awry emotionally, that something is not quite right internally during the hour. This awareness, which can also occur outside of the hour, is a signal for the therapist to look further. At a minimum, the awareness that something in not quite right internally should serve as a cue to the therapist to "watch what you do now and where you are coming from."

Even in the absence of such internal awareness, the therapist may notice that he or she is behaving in a way that seems unwise or just different from what is typical or valued. For example, a particular therapist may notice that he is talking too much and making more suggestions than usual or than he is comfortable with, or talking too little and less than he is comfortable with. Such behavioral shifts are important cues to the therapist to look inward, as well as outward—toward what is being experienced, as well as what the patient is doing that might be stirring such experience. The look inward needs to include seeking to grasp what the feelings are about in the therapist's psyche, and not just what the patient is doing or creating. In this sense, we share Eagle's (2000) view that affects are not magically transported into the therapist from the patient, no matter how primitive are the patient's defenses. Countertransference requires a "hook" in the therapist, so to speak, a soft spot that the patient's affects stimulate. Witness Kernberg's (1965) observations on analytic work with borderline patients:

> When dealing with borderline and severely regressed patients, as contrasted to those presenting symptomatic neurosis and many character disorders, the therapist tends to experience, rather soon in treatment, intensive emotional reactions having more to do with the patient's premature, intense and chaotic transference and with the therapist's capacity to withstand psychological stress and anxiety, than with any specific problem of the therapist's past. (p. 54)

What may be the soft spot when working with severely regressed patients is the therapist's difficulty withstanding emotional stress and anxiety. We view such difficulties under the heading of therapist's vulnerabilities. Any therapist will experience intense emotional reactions to borderline patients because such patients are adept at finding the soft spots in their therapists and attacking those spots. In addition, those therapists who have a limited capacity for anxiety tolerance will have even more intense countertransferences with such patients. This is probably a warning that therapists who have difficulties with anxiety tolerance probably should not be working with severely regressed and borderline patients.

Generally speaking, internal countertransference is inevitable. This is so because we therapists are all "wounded healers," no matter how well therapized or analyzed we are. The process of growing up and of living must create unresolved issues and vulnerabilities. Resolving our major thematic conflicts is certainly important, and personal therapy is a big part of that. However, we never get rid of our issues, so are always vulnerable to the patient's material. This vulnerability, though, has a positive side; for if it is not too intense and if our unresolved conflicts are not too great, the very existence of the therapist's conflicts and vulnerabilities allows for empathic connection to patients.

As we have said, internal countertransference may be helpful to the work if the therapist is able to manage and hopefully understand the source of his or her own reactions. If the therapist's unresolved problems or vulnerabilities that are being touched upon are not too great, the chances are good that the patient stimulates similar reactions in others. Thus, the therapist's internal reactions allow him or her to better understand how the patient affects others. Furthermore, because countertransference is often a reaction to the patient's underlying needs, wishes, and fears, understanding one's countertransference facilitates understanding that patient's needs, wishes, and fears within the therapeutic relationship as well as other significant relationships.

As for external countertransference, here we refer to how the internal reactions are manifested in the therapist's actual behavior with the patient. This behavior may be very subtle, it may be nonverbal, and it may not even be perceived consciously by the patient. Still, it represents acting out in one way or another the internal countertransference. When authors lament countertransference and focus on its pernicious effects, they are usually referring to external or acted-out countertransference. Is such countertransference always unhelpful or destructive? Our answer to this question is a cautious and qualified "no." At times the acting out is necessary for the therapist to see the countertransference. The aphorism, "the eye can't see itself," is apt in this respect. There are times when the therapist is blinded to internal cues of countertransference, and can only detect that something is amiss through the acting out. For example, when working with Mary, the patient described earlier, the therapist may not have had a sense of his internal countertransference until he noticed that he was responding to Mary's complaints with what he considered to be too much support, or support that was unhelpful in the last analysis. At times, such acting out has the aim of allaying the uncomfortable or painful internal countertransference reactions, and in this sense it seeks to keep countertransference feelings from awareness. Thus, it is important that the therapist pay close attention to his or her outward behavior for signs of "misbehavior."

In other instances, the patient presses so many buttons that the therapist must act out, at least to a limited degree. The case presented by Gabbard (2001) and discussed in chapter 1 is exemplary. Gabbard expressed his irritation to a patient who was being verbally abusive. Assuming that this patient stirred the therapist's aggression partly because she was hitting on areas of vulnerability (e.g., the therapist's sense of self as helpful and fears that he is not helpful enough), we may consider Gabbard's expression of irritation as countertransference. However, Gabbard's angry feelings are not only due to his vulnerabilities, but are certainly also tied to the patient's nastiness. His expression of anger in response to the patient's hostile accusation that he is only in it for the money (he replied in irritation, "that's simply not fair or accurate. I worry about you and care about your safety") helped him to see what was happening in the relationship, how the patient was affecting him, and how his reactions were unhelpful. We would consider Gabbard's reactions a rather mild acting out of countertransference that allows the therapist to grasp the relational dynamics and, more important, fosters his helping the patient explore these dynamics. Note that Gabbard did not express great hostility and was not abusive to the patient. Had he been so, that would have of course reflected more intense acting out on his part and would have been destructive. The limited acting out of countertransference exhibited by Gabbard also serves the function of demonstrating to the patient that she is in a relationship with another human being, one who has emotional frailties as all people do.

SOME KEY DISTINCTIONS

What Countertransference Is Not

As we have emphasized, a clinically meaningful and scientifically sound conception of countertransference must not be all inclusive. It must point to what is not countertransference along with what is countertransference. To begin with, we offer that countertransference is not any and all therapist reactions. Nor is it all negative or unhelpful therapist reactions. For example, it is possible to feel angry at the patient, sexually aroused by the patient, or bored with the patient without these feelings reflecting the therapist's unresolved conflicts or vulnerabilities.

These responses may at times be fully caused by the patient's behavior, his or her both overt and subtle behaviors. These reactions may be usefully grouped under the general heading of *the therapist's subjectivity*, and they are often a fundamentally important part of the therapy. They are not, however, countertransference in the way that we maintain countertransference is usefully defined.

Generally, if the reactions experienced by the therapist are intense, at least some of his or her vulnerabilities are being stirred up, although this is not always so. Each of us has experienced intense feelings in therapy that are not connected to unresolved issues, but instead are natural (at times helpful) responses to the patient's material and personhood. Feeling deeply moved or saddened by the patient's experience may not represent countertransference, but instead may represent a deeply human reaction to the emotional experience of someone who is cared about. An emotional reaction that has been greatly avoided in the clinical literature is the therapist's loving feelings toward the patient. We would maintain that these loving feelings are perhaps normal, healthy, and helpful, especially in longer term work, as the therapist comes to know the patient deeply, and in fact as the patient often comes to know the therapist deeply, even though the focus of the work is the patient's issues. The kind of loving feelings that we have in mind are captured by the Greek term, *Agape*, which refers to a nonsexualized love, a kind of brotherly or sisterly love. The concept of *love* in psychotherapy has been immensely avoided, except perhaps during the 1960s and 1970s, a time during which the humanistic movement and humanistic values were in their heyday. The avoidance, we believe, is due to our fears of acting out loving feelings in a way that takes care of the therapist's needs rather than the patient's needs. Furthermore, the connection of love to sex creates a fear in therapists that love implies sexuality. *Agape* is generally a healthy part of any good relationship, and we would not include this under the heading of countertransference. In fact, we would consider the absence of such loving feelings a more likely indication of countertransference, especially when the therapy participants have worked together on a long-term basis. In this sense, emotional neutrality (also known as indifference) is more likely to represent countertransference than is loving the patient or deeply prizing the patient.

Countertransference is also not a state or reaction in the therapist that is simply created by the patient's state or behavior, despite the fact that patients certainly do provoke states in their therapists and that such states are very important to the process, often vitally so. The now-popular idea in some psychoanalytic circles that countertransference is fully a reaction to the patient's dynamics and transference, or is composed of feelings, thoughts, and sensations that are somehow mysteriously transported from the patient's psyche to the therapist's psyche is not only mysticism that results from a lack of careful examination of the patient's actual behavior (including very subtle behavior), but it represents a subtle version of what we would call "the perfectly healed analyst" myth. In an important way, this view that countertransference is placed into the therapist abrogates the therapist's role, making the therapist not at all responsible for his or her reactions and suggesting that the therapist is but a mirror of some aspect of the patient's inner world (Eagle, 2000). The locus of causation becomes the patient, and the therapist's only job is to figure out what it is that the patient transported into him or her.

Eagle (2000) insightfully explored the fallacy of the therapist serving as a mirror whose feelings are but aspects of the patient's psyche transported into the therapist. What we would like to focus on here is how the denial of responsibility for countertransference reactions that seems reflected in this viewpoint is a repetition of the taboo against the therapist having unresolved conflicts and vulnerabilities that are a key part of the work and that must be understood if the work is to be carried out most effectively. As discussed in chapter 1, in the first half of the 20th century, theorists and practitioners avoided examinations of countertransference partly because of the view that the really good therapist or analyst had none. He or she had been effectively analyzed and was essentially without issues that may interfere with the work. Currently, within much of the psychotherapy community and particularly within certain psychoanalytic circles, we believe there is this same phobic reaction to the therapist having and attending to his or her inevitable problems and conflicts. The mirror notion that we have been discussing is in part a reflection of that phobic reaction. Instead, we believe that all therapists are wounded healers, and their work will profit greatly from attention to how their wounds become manifest in their work. The therapist makes a far greater contribution to countertransference and to his or her affective reactions in general than is implied in the mirror notion.

Given that we have sought to restrict the definition of countertransference and to delineate what countertransference is not as well as what it is, one might think that it occurs infrequently among experienced therapists. However, following the wounded healer metaphor, our view has been that we therapists all have soft spots, and that these vulnerabilities become apparent throughout our work. To be sure, it is preferable for therapists to have largely worked through their major emotional stumbling blocks, for this must make for better functioning as a therapist. But none of us is fully resolved and this lack of resolution will show itself, for better and for worse, in the work. The universal nature of countertransference, even when conservatively defined, was hinted at in a study by J. A. Hayes et al. (1998) of eight experienced and theoretically diverse therapists, who had been identified as experts by peers. These therapists each treated one patient for between 12 and 20 sessions. Most noteworthy for the present discussion, even when a conservative definition of countertransference was used, these therapists identified countertransference as operating in 80% of their 127 sessions.

We have described key distinctions between countertransference as an internal versus an external reaction, as rooted in the past versus the present, and as reflecting the therapist's issues versus the patient's affects transported into the therapist's psyche. There are some additional distinctions that must be examined for a sound understanding of countertransference. We describe these now.

Acute Versus Chronic Countertransference

The distinction was first made by Annie Reich (1951), and it has become part of most conceptions of countertransference over the years. *Acute countertransference* includes therapist responses occurring "under specific circumstances with specific patients" (A. Reich, 1951, p. 26). Reich focused on acute countertransference as representing identification with the patient. The therapist so identifies because he or she gets some emotional gratification from doing so. For example, a therapist may reinforce the patient's assertiveness as a way of satisfying her own wishes to be more assertive. Although Reich's focus was identification, acute countertransference may reflect myriad needs: (a) The therapist may reinforce submissiveness out of his need or wish to be dominant; (b) the therapist may stop listening because the patient's material is touching on a painful and unresolved current or past and repressed conflict; (c) the therapist may fall silent and become depressed when working with an assaultive patient due to the therapist's issues with his assaultive father; or (d) the therapist may begin talking too much and overadvising the patient because something in the patient's material is stirring the therapist's anxiety. All of these examples likely reflect acute countertransference, and identification with the patient may or may not be the issue.

As the name implies, chronic countertransference reflects an habitual need of the therapist, one that has likely become part of his or her self or personality structure. For example, (a) a therapist may be chronically oversupportive as a means of unconsciously gaining the support that was not sufficiently provided to her as she was growing up; (b) another therapist may see aggression in all his patients, and this may represent a projection of unresolved aggressive needs of his own; (c) a third therapist may be highly active and promote activity in all patients because of fears of her own passive side. Although there are likely patient triggers for such chronic countertransference reactions, the trigger itself is less significant than is the case for acute countertransference. The trigger for chronic countertransference is generally the frame of therapy itself rather than particulars of the patient. That is, the therapy situation is what activates the countertransference. Chronic countertransference is surely a "reaction waiting to happen."

A case example taken from the first author's supervision with a graduate student nicely captures some of the complexities of chronic countertransference. At the time of the supervision, this student was 25 years old, in the third year of her doctoral program, and in her third practicum in individual therapy. Although she appeared to have great promise as a therapist, she had a chronic tendency to underrespond to her patients. She rarely did more than reflect the patient's feelings, and mostly sat silently with her patients. Even her reflections seemed to avoid the patient's deeper feelings, of which she seemed quite aware when discussing the patient and their work during the supervision hour. Responses that required tying material together, mild confrontations, or the exploration of painful affects were avoided. Notably, outside of sessions, this therapist trainee was a well-integrated person who was liked by others and who had many friends. In other words, she was quite able to have good relationships. Here is how the student, whom we shall call Denise, understood and described her chronic countertransference:

> I don't think I can really encapsulate my chronic countertransference with one word or phrase. It is a bit of several different things—fears of rejection, failure, inadequacy, not being good enough, being wrong, and being criticized all play a part. Coming from a doctor–lawyer family, education and excelling in school have always been central to my life and self-concept. Getting As was how one got approval in my family. Bs on report cards were met with a "What happened in this class?" Getting As was seemingly the only way to get Dad's love and approval, and anything else was met with criticism, first from him and then from myself (or my internalized version of him).
>
> So, I'm an overachiever from a family with high expectations about academics—why should that result in a chronic countertransference that interferes with my ability to provide others with therapy? Perhaps ironically, my problem lies with the fact that I can't let go of the "If you only study enough, you will get the answer right and get a A" mindset. It's almost as if I "grade" my sessions, I get a score on each intervention, the number of in-

terventions, how the client responds to the interventions, whether or not the client thinks our work together is helpful, what my supervisor will say about the sessions, etcetera. If I think about it enough, I can think of plenty of places in the session where I could/should have done "better." In fact, I replay them in my mind over and over again long after the session is over.

Now, I cognitively know that there is no real "right" answer in therapy and that all terms of evaluation, like *good* and *bad*, are relative ... But knowing that there is no right answer does not keep me from feeling that paralyzing panic akin to what I feel when looking at a question on an exam and having absolutely no clue what the answer is or even how to start figuring out the answer. It's a stomach-churning, self-critical, catastrophizing, paralyzing, experience. Although I cannot remember a time when this feeling did not exist, I do remember the exact moment when it became associated with therapy. I entered my first helping-skills course feeling like I was already pretty good at helping other people when they had a problem. One day toward the end of the semester, we paired off and were instructed to role-play as clients for each other. My client began presenting her problem and paused. It was my turn to speak. I had *no idea* what to say and I felt like there was something I was *supposed* to say, as if I used to know the answer to the "question" I had been asked but had completely forgotten what it was. I felt like I was failing at doing something in which I had already considered myself skilled at, and I was getting a B or worse. My chronic countertransference has centered on the fact that I fleetingly revisit this moment every time it is my turn to speak in a therapy session.

Realizing that this anxiety about "getting a B" in doing therapy is what constrains me during sessions was of course the first step for me in overcoming this chronic countertransference problem of mine. However, at first it only served as a means to berate myself more after a session in which I was conscious of it being a problem. In fact, it just left me feeling like I'd had the ground pulled out from underneath me. I had no idea how to conceptualize my sessions without that "must-get-an-A" mindset. I hated that I did this to myself but had no idea what else to do.

This student successfully overcame much of her chronic countertransference through her personal therapy. Our observations are that because chronic countertransference can be so pervasive within one's personality, personal therapy is likely to be necessary to work this through. In the case of Denise, the chronic countertransference was of a degree and kind that work as a therapist was seriously impeded. It should be noted that we often hear the question, "Is it countertransference or lack of experience that is at play?" Our reply usually is that it is both, and that countertransference is usually greater with less experienced therapists. Thankfully, we have less countertransference and learn how to better manage countertransference as we develop and gain experience as therapists. Personal therapy is an important part of that therapeutic development.

Countertransference as Projection Versus Countertransference as Emotional Reaction

As we noted earlier, it is common to consider countertransference as representing the therapist's transference. In this sense, feelings, attitudes, and impulses connected to significant others early in the therapist's life are displaced onto the patient (Freud, 1912/1959a, b; Gelso & Hayes, 1998; Luborsky & Crits-Christoph, 1990). Although this certainly does happen in therapy, as we have said, it seems to be more often the case that material from the patient touches upon areas of unresolved conflict or vulnerability, which arouses defensive reactions in the therapist. The critical, hard-to-please patient may stir unresolved conflicts in the therapist around not being good enough. Although these feelings likely have their basis in early significant relationships, it does not seem to be the case generally that those early figures are displaced or projected onto the patient. More likely, feelings about not being good enough get aroused in the therapist, and these are dealt with in either therapeutic or countertherapeutic ways in the treatment. We suspect that the vastly different roles of therapist and patient are centrally implicated in the ways in which transference and countertransference operate. Because the patient is in the help-receiving role, he or she is more likely to make projections onto the therapist from significant others who were responsible for the patient's well-being (e.g., parents). Because the therapist is in the help-offering role, projections and displacements of this sort are less likely. Instead, it is more likely that patient material triggers responses tied to unresolved issues in the therapist without the involvement of displacement and projection.

Because it is being suggested that countertransference is not usually the therapist's transference in the sense of implicating projections and displacements onto the patient, and because we noted earlier that countertransference is not necessarily a reaction to the patient's transference, the reader may wonder why we maintain the term countertransference at all. If neither the patient nor the therapist may be exhibiting transference, why call the therapist's reactions countertransference? Our answer is twofold. First, when countertransference is being exhibited, there is ordinarily some degree of transference occurring in the room. Either the patient is transferring onto the therapist or the therapist is transferring onto the patient (even though we think this does not occur in countertransference, as has been implied often in the psychoanalytic literature), and in this sense, transference is usually implicated in one way or another. Furthermore, even when the therapist's reactions that stem from unresolved conflicts or vulnerabilities are not transferential, and when they are not a reaction to the patient's transference, it seems worth maintaining the customary term rather than creating a new one.

Countertransference as Too Much, Too Little, Too Positive, or Too Negative

Like transference, countertransference is often a matter of excess. The therapist who becomes bored, withdraws from the patient, daydreams about other relationships or events, maintains emotional neutrality throughout, or does not feel any caring for the patient is likely involved in countertransference. We would consider these reactions as underinvolvement. But too much involvement likely reflects countertransference as well. The therapist who must rush in to solve the patient's problems, the one who loses all neutrality and sides with the patient in nearly all of the patient's struggles with nearly everyone, and the therapist who spends too much time out of the hour thinking or fantasizing about the patient—all of these seem to be expressing their countertransference in terms of overinvolvement.

Just as the therapist can be over- or underinvolved, so can he or she display positive or negative countertransference. This distinction has been supported by factor analytic research (Freidman & Gelso, 2001). Thus, countertransference is likely at work when the therapist expresses hostility and other negative reactions toward the patient. Not as obvious but just as important, positive feelings that come from the therapist's issues can hinder the work. Thus, the therapist can care too much, be too supportive, and kindly allow the patient to totally run the hour without challenge.

These two related dimensions of overinvolvement–underinvolvement and positive–negative countertransference have been theorized for many years. Recently they have also been pointed to in qualitative research intensely studying small numbers of patient–therapist dyads (Gelso, Hill, Mohr, Rochlen, & Zack, 1999; Hayes et al., 1998; Hill, Nutt-Williams, Heaton, Thompson, & Rhodes, 1996). A look at some of the key findings is instructive.

Underinvolvement was noted in some of the cases reported by Hill and her collaborators (1996) of therapeutic impasse that brought therapy to an end. In one long-term therapy case (300 sessions), the impasse revolved around a feeling that the therapy was going in circles. At the time of the impasse, the client had a strong wish for the therapist to offer advice about whether to get married again. Yet this client continually rejected the therapist's perspective on his [the client's] life. This was a most difficult client, and as the impasse unfolded:

> Dr. K felt frustrated, trapped, and disappointed by the impasse. She wondered if she had been too passive, avoiding a more confrontive, active, and directive stance out of fear of becoming controlling like the client's mother. She also recognized that she had her own personal issues about aggression (e.g., she became defensive and felt like running out of the room when the client verbally attacked her). (p. 213)

Although one could never know the precise nature of the countertransference behavior from the brief example presented by Hill et al. (1996), it does appear that the therapist withdrew from the patient, and became underinvolved. Similarly, in a study of self-reports of eight seasoned therapists, each working with one client, J. A. Hayes et al. (1998) noted that all of the therapists experienced avoidance reactions of one kind or another during parts of their work with their client:

> For example, one therapist, who had a need to "look good" professionally, distanced himself emotionally from a client with whom he felt stuck. Another therapist, who had unresolved issues around being childless, said in one postsession interview, "it may be a matter of countertransference that I got a little bit bored about her long-winded tale about the daughter." (p. 475)

As for overinvolvement, in their study of successful long-term dynamic therapy, Gelso et al. (1999) noted that some therapists reported being overgratifying (e.g., therapist overpraising the client) and overly responsible for taking care of their clients, as well as for client improvement. We should note, though, that this area of therapist overinvolvement has been difficult for researchers to pin down, despite the fact that we have encountered overinvolvement with some frequency in our clinical supervision and have observed it in ourselves at times, along with the fact that it appears prominently in the literature as one of the key manifestations of countertransference. In an effort to study overinvolvement, for example, Gelso and his collaborators (Gelso, Fassinger, Gomez, & Latts, 1995) developed a measure based on judges' ratings of therapist-trainees' responses to audiotaped clients. Two findings were of note: (a) the therapist-trainees tended to score very high on the measure, indicating that overinvolvement was a common difficulty of these trainees; but (b) the measure had marginal reliability at best.

Clearly we need an effective method of assessing overinvolvement empirically and studying its causes and effects. The main difficulty has revolved around differentiating genuine countertransference from therapist activity and involvement levels that are theoretically based. For example, what a traditional psychoanalyst might see as overinvolvement that is likely countertransference based, a cognitive-behavioral therapist or a feminist therapist might see as appropriate and helpful support and advocacy on the part of the therapist.

As for positive and negative countertransference, both of these were noted in the three qualitative studies. J. A. Hayes et al. (1998), for example, labeled one of the four categories of therapist countertransference *negative feelings*. To one degree or another, these occurred in all therapists and they could have the effect of either increasing or decreasing the distance between the participants. Negative feelings in the Hayes et al. (1998) study included anger and frustration; sadness; inadequacy; anxiety or pressure; feelings such as guilt, envy, and pity; anticipating negative feelings; and guarding against negative feelings and behaviors. We should note here that some of these affects might also be labeled *positive countertransference*. For example, the therapist who experienced an "empathic sadness" with her client and described "reaching" for something in the client may be experiencing a positively valenced countertransference while also experiencing what Hayes et al. (1998) termed negative feelings, that is, sadness.

What is clear from each of these three qualitative studies, as well as quantitative research (Friedman & Gelso, 2000; Ligiero & Gelso, 2002), is that positively valenced feelings the therapist has for the client may also be rooted in countertransference, that these feelings may help or hinder the process, and that therapists needs to monitor and manage their positive feelings as well as their negative feelings. Observe the therapist in J. A. Hayes et al. (1998), who tended to worry about his own children's safety, and who thus empathized deeply with his client when she described fears of not being able to protect her children from harm. In the therapist's own words, "I understand the fear and worry and how terrible losing a kid would be for me, you know. And I certainly at times in my life have an ongoing fantasy about the atom bomb being dropped and what would I do and what route would I get out of the city, you know ... so I have some, I guess mostly just empathy of that situation" (p. 475). In this case, although the therapist's issues around his children's safety, and their perhaps unconscious antecedents, appeared to deepen his empathic understanding of his client, these internal and external reactions required understanding, monitoring, and management. Without that, it would be easy to see how this empathy could transform into a kind of overinvolvement that was too protective of the client (and her child), and in the end aimed at protecting the therapist from anxiety about losses rather than helping the client resolve her own problems.

Our research (Friedman & Gelso, 2000; J. A. Hayes et al., 1998; Ligiero & Gelso, 2002) tell us that although positively valenced countertransference looks more beneficial and helpful on the surface, its effects can be as damaging as negatively valenced countertransference if not understood, monitored, and managed.

Countertransference as a Two-Person Versus a One-Person Phenomenon

There has been much writing over the past decade or so about whether psychoanalysis is best seen and practiced as a two-person psychology or a one-person psychology. This debate is usually framed in terms of classical psychoanalysis (e.g., drive and ego psychology) in contrast to psychoanalytic self-psychology and object-relations theories, including those labeled *intersubjective* (Stolorow, Brandchaft, & Atwood, 1987), *relational* (Mitchell & Aron, 1999), and *interpersonal* (Anchin & Kiesler, 1982). Classical analysis is seen as a one-person psychology (by the others), whereas the other approaches we have noted view themselves as two-person psychologies. As implied, this distinction is made usually by those who are not classicists.

How and in what ways are therapy approaches one-person or two-person psychologies? The one-person psychologies focus on the patient. It is the patient who seeks treatment for problems, and who carries defenses, dynamics, and psychopathology with him or her into the treatment. The patient also carries transference proclivities into treatment. The analyst's job, stated simply and simplistically, is to grasp the patient's unconscious and to offer interpretations aimed at rendering insight in the patient. Insight into the transference is especially valued. The analyst's role is to maintain analytic neutrality rather than identify with the patient's impulses, superego, or neurotic ego. The analyst must also maintain ambiguity, presenting him- or herself in a rather gray color so as to not intrude on the developing transference. If and when the analyst's personal conflicts enter the therapeutic field, these must be analyzed and worked through so that they do not impinge upon the developing transference. In this one-person scenario, the analyst stays out of the drama created by the patient's pathology, except as the patient creates distorted images of the analyst that are displacements from early objects in his or her life, and reflect unresolved conflicts that are the core of the patient's pathology. Few if any therapists would adhere to this position in today's world of psychotherapy.

As Gabbard (2001) tells us, "theorists from diverse persuasions have converged on the idea that, to some extent, countertransference is always a joint creation involving contributions from both clinician and patient" (p. 989). In this sense, the large majority of today's therapists are two-person psychologists. At the same time, differences manifest themselves in terms of the relative emphasis given to each of the participants. Our conception is that in the continual interplay of therapist and patient, each brings his or her own issues, conflicts, vulnerabilities, and ways of being to the therapeutic table. As for the countertransference, some therapists bring chronic countertransference issues to the table, and these will be enacted with virtually any patient with whom these therapists interact. These same therapists, as well as all other therapists, possess certain vulnerabilities and unresolved issues that come to the fore only when stirred by the patient and his or her behavior and issues. The manner in which these more acute countertransferences emerge, their intensity and duration, is shaped by the particulars of the therapeutic relationship, including the person and behavior of the patient.

We have said little about how the therapist's conflicts, vulnerabilities, and ways of being affect the patient, although everything we have just noted about the patient's influence on the therapist can be said for the therapist's influence on the patient. This two-person or intersubjective push and pull goes on within the context of two separate people, so there are three forces operating: the two individuals and what they each brings to the table, and the relationship, that is, their intersubjectivity, or what Ogden (1994) referred to as the "analytic third."

Our two-person emphasis entails a great deal of mutual influence. And yet the therapist must be ever mindful that this mutuality does not imply symmetry. The patient is in the help-seeking role, is paying usually for treatment, and is in a situation in which he or she shares very intimate and delicate feelings, thoughts, and experiences. Whatever his or her theoretical persuasion, the therapist is in the help-giving role, is providing psychotherapy, and is bound by a set of ethical standards. The boundaries implied by these roles are vital to the therapeutic enterprise and must always be maintained. This is especially so at a time in which the therapist's emotional involvement and availability in all theoretical approaches are taken for granted. The dire problems that can emerge when mutuality is transformed into symmetry are disturbingly portrayed in the following vignette presented by Gabbard (2001):

A middle-aged male therapist was seeing Freda, a young patient with avoidant personality disorder, in twice-weekly dynamic psychotherapy. The patient was describing her anxieties about dating and told her therapist that she was convinced [that] she would be rejected by men. She said that men did not find her sexually desirable. The therapist said that she was obviously an attractive woman and that he was sure that men would find her desirable. Freda asked her therapist why he felt so sure. He responded, "Because I find you sexually desirable." The patient blushed and looked anxious. She said to the therapist, "I don't think you're supposed to say things like that to me." The therapist responded, "There is no problem in my expressing my feelings here. I'm a man and you're a woman, even if we're in the roles of therapist and patient." Freda told the therapist, "But knowing that you have sexual feelings for me makes me feel unsafe in here." The therapist then responded, "But I'm sure that you would not allow me to act on them." With a worried look on her face, the patient said, "This is just like what happened with my dad. He was always wanting to hug me and touch me, and I always had to be the one to set limits." She fell silent until the end of the hour. She never returned for another session.

Despite the mutuality involved in the therapeutic relationship, this relationship is not symmetrical in the sense that each can freely express feelings toward the other and each can take the role of the other. The confusion of mutuality and symmetry on the part of the therapist is a major countertransference breach that is bound to have disastrous effects, regardless of the therapist's theoretical orientation.

THE STRUCTURE OF COUNTERTRANSFERENCE

Based on theory (Hayes, 1995), and research (J. A. Hayes & Gelso, 2001; J. A. Hayes et al., 1998), we believe it useful to conceptualize countertransference as containing certain structural elements, or what we refer to as Origins, Triggers, Manifestations, Effects, and Management. These represent the key elements in understanding countertransference, where it comes from, what causes it, how it shows itself, its effects on process and outcome, and finally how the therapist can manage countertransference so that it aids treatment. Now we briefly describe each element, and in chapter 6, we discuss in some detail the empirical research around each of these five elements.

Origins: Where Does Countertransference Come From?

As we have discussed, countertransference originates from within the therapist—from his or her unresolved conflicts and vulnerabilities.

Countertransference may originate from these conflicts and vulnerabilities tied to any point in the therapist's life, and we have found it useful to view the origins of countertransference as developmental in nature. The roots of this phenomenon may usually be traced back to issues from the therapist's childhood. Usually these roots are not very obvious to the therapist. Often origins are themselves derivatives of early conflict. For example, the therapist's conflicts about not being "good enough" to help the patient may be a derivative of earlier conflicts around being a disappointment to his parents or not receiving good enough parenting in his or her childhood. As this example demonstrates, countertransferences are usually multilayered (J. A. Hayes & Gelso, 2001) in the sense that the therapist experiences conflict or vulnerability in the hour with his or her patient, and this conflict exists in the therapist's current life. Yet the origin of the conflict is usually much earlier.

Although the roots of countertransference are ordinarily found in the therapist's childhood, this is not always the case, as discussed earlier in this chapter. There are many emotional conflicts that occur in the now, exist in the now, and do not have early antecedents. The therapist may have experienced a traumatic loss in the present or the recent past, for example, loss of a relationship, loss of a job, loss of status. The patient's losses may thus stir affects tied to the lack of resolution of these losses. To be sure, the frequency, intensity, and duration of these affects in the therapist may be rooted in earlier losses, but at times they may not be or it may be begging the question to search for antecedents. One can think of many losses and other difficulties that create great pain in which this pain is a part of the human condition rather than being a result of unresolved issues in childhood. When such losses occur, it is much more challenging for the therapist to work effectively with a patient who is experiencing similar losses and/or affects.

Triggers: What Happens in the Hour to Precipitate Countertransference?

Triggers are therapy events or patient qualities that touch upon or bring out the therapist's unresolved conflicts or vulnerabilities. Researchers have looked for patient behaviors that trigger countertransference for a long time. Typically studied are patient presenting problems (e.g., rape, HIV infection, same-sex relationship problems), and presenting styles (e.g., hostility, dependency, seductiveness). This work has not proven to be very fruitful and few clear-cut findings have emerged from it. This is likely due to the very mutuality that we earlier discussed. That is, which particular patient attributes and behaviors serve as triggers to countertransference depends a great deal on the particular vulnerabilities of the therapist. Cast in terms of our structural conception of countertransference, one could view the causes of countertransference as reflecting an interaction of Origins and Triggers. We refer to this as the *countertransference interaction hypothesis*. An example of this occurred in two of our laboratory studies (Gelso et al, 1995; J. A. Hayes & Gelso, 1993), in which it was found that the client's sexual orientation had no effect on countertransference in general. However, when the therapist's own fears and conflicts around homosexuality were taken into account, we found that these powerfully predicted countertransference feelings and behaviors with gay and lesbian clients.

The countertransference interaction hypothesis has been supported in a number of laboratory and field studies. These are examined in chapter 6. The key point here is that it is generally not useful to think of classes of patient triggers for countertransference. Instead, we must nearly always look at how client attributes and behaviors interact with the therapist's vulnerabilities and issues if we are to understand the triggers for countertransference. Each therapist needs to reflect upon what client material or attributes trigger his or her own conflicts and vulnerabilities as a basic step in managing countertransference. These triggers may reflect the patient's individual qualities, qualities tied to culture, or group membership (e.g., race, ethnicity, gender, sexual orientation). Most likely the triggers involve some combination of these factors. But the bottom line is, again, how these patient attributes interact with the therapist's issues.

An example of how the countertransference interaction hypothesis operates in the area of ethnicity and culture may be seen in the work of a seasoned and highly gifted therapist with a substantial background in multicultural psychology.

> The client was a Colombian woman who suffered from panic attacks, and the therapist's background was also Colombian. Racially, both were White. The client clearly could have benefited from desensitization therapy, and the therapist ordinarily referred to other therapists for such work. In this case, however, the therapist conducted the treatment herself. On reflection after termination, the therapist believed that she treated the case because of her identification with the client as a Colombian. The therapist also believed she may not have been doing enough analytic work (her preferred orientation) about how the panic came to be. She felt this avoidance of analytic work was due to the fact that the panic likely was rooted in the widespread violence and terror in Colombia, and this would be painful for both client and therapist to explore. Thus, the focus on behavioral work may have reflected a posttraumatic avoidance on the part of both therapist and client. (Gelso & Mohr, 2001, p. 65)

Parenthetically, this case example also demonstrates how positive countertransference can be just as problematic as negative countertransference if not understood and managed. Helping clients avoid painful feelings, in this case around culture, may be as harmful as the acting out of negative countertransference.

Manifestations: How Does Countertransference Show Itself?

Countertransference may be manifested by the therapist in any or all of three forms: affects, behaviors, or cognitions. None of these in and of themselves indicate countertransference. Instead they are signs for the therapist that he or she needs to look inward to see what is being stirred up and why. The affect that seems most fundamental to countertransference is therapist anxiety. When therapists perceive aspects of the clinical situation to be personally threatening, anxiety is a natural consequence. Indeed, clinical wisdom has long held that therapist anxiety is a warning signal, urging the therapist to look to the relationship and look inward for something that may be awry. And research has supported clinical lore; anxiety is the most common therapist affective reaction when personal conflicts are stirred in the treatment. Of course, many affective states, including anger, sadness, excitement, sexual arousal, boredom, and happiness may be indicative of countertransference. In fact, when J. A. Hayes and his colleagues (1998) studied the postsession interviews of eight experienced therapists over 127 sessions, they found that the majority of therapists felt angry, bored, sad, nurturing, and inadequate in as many as half their sessions.

In keeping with our conception of countertransference, it must be clarified that none of these affects necessarily indicates the existence of countertransference. Instead, affects that are experienced as incongruent or different from the therapist's usual emotional state in therapy are an invitation for the therapist to introspect as to their origins.

The usual manner in which countertransference behavior manifests itself is through the therapist's avoidance of, withdrawal from, or underinvolvement with the patient and his or her material. This can take many more specific forms; changing the topic, not responding to the threatening material, falling silent, and daydreaming are common behavioral manifestations of avoidance and withdrawal. At the other end of the continuum, overinvolvement may manifest itself behaviorally in terms of too much talking, too many suggestions, too much support, too much affection, and excessive reassurance. As is the case with affective manifestations, both under- and overinvolving behaviors are not in and of themselves necessarily indicative of countertransference. Whether they are or not depends on what in the therapist stimulates these behaviors.

A third behavioral manifestation that is more assuredly indicative of countertransference revolves around therapist aggression. Critical and attacking behavior on the part of the therapist is most often a sign of countertransference, even when the patient's behavior is provoking. This is especially so when therapist hostility reaches a high level of intensity.

Countertransference may also be manifested cognitively. For many authors, the cognitive concept of *distortion* lies at the very heart of countertransference (Hayes & Gelso, 2001). Although we do not suggest that distortion of aspects of the patient is the most common manifestation of countertransference, these distortions surely do happen. For example, in one of the earliest studies of countertransference, Cutler (1958) found that when patients talked about material related to therapists' unresolved issues, therapists tended to misperceive the frequency with which patients talked about those topics. Other studies support this idea—therapists are more likely to under- or overestimate the sheer frequency of patient material when it touches upon their own issues. Such therapist distortions may have a far-reaching impact on the work, including stimulating therapists to bring treatment to a premature ending! (J. A. Hayes & Gelso, 2001).

Effects: What Does Countertransference Do to the Process and Outcome of Therapy?

In an early review of the research literature on countertransference approximately three decades ago, B. A. Singer and Luborsky (1977) drew this conclusion:

> *Perhaps the most clear-cut and important area of congruence between the clinical and quantitative literatures is the widely agreed-upon position that uncontrolled countertransference has an adverse effect on therapy outcome.* Not only does it have a markedly detrimental influence on the therapist's technique and interventions, but it also interferes with the optimal understanding of the patient. (p. 49)

Our reviews of the effect of countertransference behavior on both treatment process and outcome lend credence to these early conclusions (Gelso & Hayes, 2002; J. A. Hayes & Gelso, 2001). It seems clear that countertransference that is not understood, controlled, and managed by the therapist will injure the treatment. The empirical literature has much to say about the ways in which unmanaged countertransference hinders the process. We have much to say about this in chapter 6, but for now we only summarize that unmanaged countertransference appears to be part of avoiding the patient's feelings, recalling the content of sessions inaccurately, and becoming overinvolved in the patient's problems. Furthermore, it appears to be related to poor patient–therapist alliances and to clinical supervisors' evaluations of effectiveness.

And yet we have also noted earlier that countertransference has the potential to deeply benefit the therapy. The double helix of hindrance and potential benefit is underscored in two examples from J. A. Hayes and colleagues (1998) qualitative study of eight psychotherapies referred to earlier. As for hindering effects, they point to the therapist who was too immersed in her countertransference issues of strength and independence to connect with her dependent patient. On the positive side, though, they noted the therapist who was able to make use of her countertransference-based needs to nurture and be a good parent by appropriately supporting and being patient with her client.

So countertransference can be for better or worse, depending on how it is managed by the therapist. We now view briefly the work on countertransference management.

Countertransference Management: What Allows Countertransference to Facilitate?

Chapter 5 is devoted entirely to countertransference management. Here we provide an overview of these facilitative factors. Our theory of countertransference management specifies five factors that underlie and aid the therapist in his or her quest to use countertransference wisely. The first factor is *therapist self-insight*. We are reminded of Plato's simple maxim: "Know thyself." Stated in a more elaborate form, "A knowledge of my propensities will hopefully keep me from falling too deeply into countertransference reactions or at least help me to deal with them more swiftly, before they have done any major harm" (Robertiello & Schoenewolf, 1987, p. 289).

The therapist who values and seeks insight into his or her own workings is likely to be the therapist who will make the best use of countertransference. This is the therapist who is going to stop and reflect upon what is going on internally when his or her feelings seem off base, or just do not seem quite right. When the insightful therapist exhibits actions that do not seem to have the intended effect or seem amiss, that therapist wants to know where he or she is coming from.

The second factor in countertransference management is *self-integration*. Here we refer to the therapist's possession of a unified, basically intact character structure, which includes boundaries that are solid enough that he or she had a good sense of "where the patient stops and he or she starts." At the same time, these boundaries are not so solid that the therapist cannot put him- or herself aside, at least partially, and enter into the patient's world. Stated differently, the therapist is effective at "merging with and separating from the patient, participating with him and then standing back and observing his participation" (Gorkin, 1987, p. 80).

The third factor is *empathy*. In lay terms, we refer here to the therapist's ability to temporarily put parts of the self aside and climb into the other's shoes. More technically, we can think of empathy as vicarious, partial identification, or as the term favored by the fonder of psychoanalytic self-psychology, Heinz Kohut (1977), *vicarious introspection*. Empathy permits the therapist to maintain his or her focus on the patient rather than being absorbed or overwhelmed by his or her own issues. Also, by maintaining attunement to the patient's feelings, therapists are less likely to act out based on their own needs.

Fourth, *anxiety management* is a key constituent of countertransference management. Here we refer to the ability to recognize, tolerate, and even learn from one's anxiety. Note that we are not suggesting that the therapist eliminate anxiety. Instead, allowing the self to know or be in touch with anxiety, and then working to grasp what it is about is fundamental to good anxiety management. The good therapist does not run away from anxiety, but in a certain sense embraces it.

Finally, *conceptualizing skills* are a key constituent of countertransference management. Here we refer to the cognitive processing of both the patient's dynamics and the dynamics of the therapeutic relationship. In this process, the therapist's knowledge of theory and ability to apply theory to the therapeutic relationship is important. We believe that therapists who can use theory to understand what is happening in the treatment hour, regardless of the particulars of that theory, will do a better job of dealing with their own vulnerabilities that are inevitably stimulated in the treatment hour.

CONCLUSION

In this chapter, we have presented a conception of countertransference that is similar to the four main conceptions that have developed over the years, but also different from each of these. We have defined countertransference and clarified, too, what it is not. We have discussed key distinctions that must be attended to if countertransference itself is to be understood deeply. And we have examined the interplay of countertransference origins, triggers, manifestations, effects, and management in the work of psychotherapy.

In discussing the elements of a good theory of countertransference, we have pointed to the importance of understanding its operation across key theories of therapy, although we have had little to say about this so far. As noted, because countertransference originates in psychoanalytic thought in no way implies that it belongs to psychoanalysis and is a key construct only in that theory. Instead it is a universal in psychotherapy because therapists of all persuasions have soft spots that can be and are touched upon in their work. But how might countertransference operate in diverse theories? We address this important question in chapter 3.

3

Countertransference Within Different Theoretical Stances

This chapter addresses conceptualizations of countertransference within three major approaches to psychotherapy. The origins of these theoretical systems may be broadly construed as reflecting three primary components of human beings: the physical, the intellectual, and the emotional. The theoretical patterns to which these components correspond, respectively, are the behavioral, psychoanalytic, and humanistic approaches. Of course, transformations within these systems over time have yielded a blending of emphases so that, for instance, the behavioral tradition has incorporated cognitive and, to a lesser degree, emotional elements into its theory. Nonetheless, therapists who work within a theoretical framework that emphasizes action, insight, or emotions may be susceptible to vulnerabilities in one or both of the other areas. As Jung postulated, that which is relegated to the shadow accumulates energy and eventually exerts control over one's behavior.

By way of illustration, a cognitive-behavioral colleague of ours has a general proclivity for telling people what to do, both in her life in general and with her patients. There is good reason for her directive nature, of course. As a child, she experienced a fair amount of instability within her family and coped by controlling her environment as best she could. As an adult, in both her personal and professional relationships, by taking charge she probably gets reinforced. She works prescriptively and, given her positive reputation, very effectively with her adolescent patients; she provides wise direction and advice to colleagues who seek consultation from her; and she helps organize professional functions in the community. However, based on both social and professional interactions with her, it is probably fair to say that she is not particularly attuned to nuances within the emotional realm. In social situations, she prefers to talk about facts and observations, and in case discussions she sometimes struggles to recognize what is transpiring on an emotional level for her patients as well as herself. Following interactions, one is often left with a sense of having not connected fully or deeply with her. Our aim here is not to deride a fellow therapist and acquaintance, but rather to note that her understandable proclivity for cognitive-behavioral work may make her prone to missing emotional cues in therapy, both her patients' and her own.

Just as emotions may be soft spots for some cognitive-behavioral therapists, we have supervised a number of humanistically oriented trainees who at times empathize so strongly with their patients' affect that they have difficulty stepping back and effectively conceptualizing patient concerns. For these therapists, the emotional domain tends to constitute figure and the cognitive realm is ground. Again, much good can result from empathizing deeply with patients, and it is hard to conceive of any kind of therapy going well without at least some emotional empathy from the therapist. However, for therapy to proceed optimally, conceptualization skills are critical. In fact, one study of countertransference management and outcome found that therapists' conceptualizing abilities were positively related to patient improvement (Gelso, Latts, Gomez, & Fassinger, 2002). The ability to conceptualize may be especially important when the therapy becomes bogged down or altogether stuck. At these times, an understanding of the factors contributing to an impasse can provide direction for getting unstuck.

COUNTERTRANSFERENCE IN THE COGNITIVE-BEHAVIORAL APPROACHES

The behaviorally and cognitively oriented approaches traditionally have devoted little attention to the psychotherapy relationship and even less to countertransference. Given the paucity of interest in countertransference reflected in the cognitive-behavioral literature, one might conclude that it is not considered an important construct or that countertransference simply does not occur in this form of treatment. Whereas there may be some truth to the former, we believe the latter is patently untrue. All therapists, by virtue of their humanity, are prone to having their conflicts and vulnerabilities stimulated by patients, regardless of their theoretical orientation. It may be that, because cognitive-behavioral treatment depends more upon technical than relational factors to promote change, countertransference affects the process and outcome of this form of therapy less than in other approaches. However, it would be a mistake to conclude that countertransference exerts no or minimal influence on the course of cognitive-behavioral treatment. Theoreticians are increasingly recognizing this to be the case, as we soon discuss.

Some cognitive-behavioral theorists, perhaps not surprisingly, prefer to reframe countertransference in other terms. Rudd and Joiner (1997) favor the phrase "therapeutic belief system" rather than "countertransference" because it is less tied to a psychoanalytic heritage and framework, with all of its attendant assumptions. For example, the psychoanalytic emphasis on the unconscious is inconsistent with basic tenets of cognitive therapy, such as the assumption that thoughts can be readily accessed and known and that the present is more important than the past. Interestingly, however, a consensus is emerging among cognitive therapists that a *cognitive unconscious* exists and exerts influence on behavior (Dowd & Courchaine, 1996). Nonetheless, in terms of both theory and practice, cognitive behaviorists still stress patient material that is close to the surface and near to the present.

Historically, in the most radical forms of behaviorism, the role of the therapist was virtually negligible. The therapist functioned essentially as a technician and, as long as techniques were implemented properly, it almost did not matter who was applying them. In fact,behavioral interventions were developed that did not even require a therapist to be present, such as tape-recorded instructions for desensitization (Lang, Melamed, & Hart, 1970). The current proliferation and documented effectiveness of self-help books also invites curiosity about the very necessity of a therapist, at least for certain problems (Scogin, 2003). The recent trend toward "manualized" treatment raises further questions about the role of the therapist. To the extent that treatment can be standardized, the person of the therapist, including her or his vulnerabilities, conflicts, and soft spots, may be less relevant to the delivery of services. However, we doubt whether therapy can ever become so formulaic that the person of the therapist is, or even should be, removed from the equation. Furthermore, as Wampold (2001) cogently argues, scientific evidence presently does not demonstrate the superiority of manualized treatments, and moreover, therapist factors account for a greater share of variance in outcome than do treatment-specific factors (e.g., techniques). Strupp's (1958) wisdom from a bygone era is pertinent to the current debate:

> It is clear that therapeutic techniques are not applied *in vacuo*, and that they are differentially affected by factors in the therapist's personality. His performance is determined—in part, at least—by the way in which he perceives the patient's behavior, interprets its meaning in the framework of his clinical experience *and* his own personality, and the way in which this meaning is reflected in his response. (p. 35)

As noted previously, the therapy relationship, and the therapist's role within that relationship, has been afforded increased prominence in cognitive and behavioral approaches. Goldfried and Davidson (1982) make this point emphatically: "Any behavior therapist who maintains that principles of learning and social influence are all one needs to know in order to bring about behavior change is out of contact with clinical reality" (p. 55). They go on to note that, although behaviorists view patients' problems

> In relation to principles of conditioning, reinforcement, social influence, and the like, these concepts involve the therapists' scientific meta-language and are not descriptive or prescriptive of the way he should interact with his client. The truly skillful behavior therapist is one who can both conceptualize problems behaviorally and make the necessary translations so that he interacts in a warm and empathic manner with his client. (p. 56)

Goldfried and Davidson underscore their point by noting that research indicates that the therapeutic effectiveness of techniques is enhanced when they are delivered in the context of a positive relationship.

In addition to enhancing the effectiveness of techniques, another reason why more attention is being paid to the therapy relationship in cognitive-behavioral approaches is that therapists with these orientations increasingly are dealing with patients suffering from highly complex disorders requiring long-term treatments. Linehan's (1993) dialectical behavior therapy, for example, grew out of her work with suicidal patients, many of who had borderline personality disorder. Because of the longer term nature of the work with these difficult patients, the therapy relationship is likely to undergo periods of stress and strain, requiring the therapist's attention to and skillful handling of relationship dynamics. This interpersonal dexterity is especially important in dealing with suicidal patients, because they can be prone to perceiving therapists as critical and blaming, thus increasing the risk that they will terminate therapy prematurely (Maltsberger & Buie, 1989; Rudd, Joiner, & Rajab,

1995). Working with borderline patients, whether they are actively suicidal or not, also presents significant challenges for therapists. Because they typically have a history of neglect, individuals with borderline personality disorder become highly skilled at reading their environments, perceiving others' vulnerabilities, and provoking strong reactions from others. This behavior serves the functions of determining others' limits, maintaining some form of engagement with another, or creating interpersonal distance. When working with borderline patients, then, therapists can expect to have frequent and intense countertransference reactions (Gabbard & Wilkinson, 2000). These reactions need to be skillfully managed for therapy of any theoretical persuasion to be effective (see chap. 5 for theory and research on countertransference management).

To reiterate, effective cognitive-behavioral therapy is not simply a matter of the therapist's employing techniques derived from principles of learning. This portrayal is a far too basic, and in fact misleading, characterization of cognitive-behavioral therapy. The manner in which therapists perceive, diagnose, conceptualize, treat, and otherwise respond to patients is to a large degree subjective, manuals notwithstanding, and that subjectivity is in part influenced by therapists' conflicts and vulnerabilities. Patients inevitably will evoke countertransference reactions from therapists, even when treatment is not centered on the therapy relationship (as it is, say, in interpersonal therapy) and even when the relationship is considered secondary to techniques as a mechanism for change. Consequently, countertransference management is critical for cognitive-behavioral therapists, regardless of the patient populations with whom they work. From our perspective, the topic of managing one's personal reactions to patients usually is addressed insufficiently, if at all, in treatment manuals and other forms of training for cognitive-behavioral therapists.

Cognitive-Behavioral Construals of Countertransference Phenomena

Originally a psychoanalytic construct, countertransference has been recast in interesting ways by cognitive-behavioral theorists. As one might expect, learning theory is used to explain both the origins and the manifestations of countertransference. In terms of the causes of countertransference, Ellis (2001) notes that countertransference is defined in Corsini's (1999) *Dictionary of Psychology* in cognitive terms, as "schemas deriving from one's personal history" (p. 1015). Similarly, countertransference has been conceptualized by cognitive-behavioral theorists as originating in a therapist's scripts, prototypes, irrational beliefs, and automatic thoughts (Ellis, 2001; Layden, Newman, Freeman, & Morse, 1993; J. L. Singer, Sincoff, & Kolligian, 1989). J. L. Singer et al. (1989) note that "schemas represent the mechanisms underlying the hidden agendas that we all—therapist and patient alike—bring to each life experience and situation" (p. 347). In particular, therapists' schemas about the self, about situations (i.e., scripts), and about others (i.e., prototypes) enable the therapist to organize information, anticipate events, and behave efficiently. However, as research on information processing has demonstrated, these same schemas make the therapist susceptible to egocentric biases, selective attention, and faulty heuristics, all of which can serve as the basis for countertransference reactions. Furthermore, Ellis (2001) points out that a cognitive-behavioral therapist's needs (e.g., to be respected and appreciated) can interfere with the attainment of therapy goals (e.g., when the therapist fails to push patients to change). Ellis (2001) provides a rich example from his own work to illustrate the point.

Ellis describes his enjoyment working with a young, attractive, bright woman who, in only a few sessions, readily put his relational-emotive behavior therapy (REBT) principles into practice. After making considerable progress on her presenting problem, a second issue emerged related to the patient's highly critical stance toward romantic partners. Ellis pointed out and challenged her low frustration tolerance with men but made little headway. Fearing he might lose her as a patient—and the pleasure he received from working with her—Ellis backed away from confronting the patient further. She persisted in her critical ways until eventually she lost what had been a fairly healthy romantic relationship. Despite her attempts to regain the relationship, the patient was unable to do so. The patient then turned on Ellis—and rightly so in his eyes—for abandoning his attempts to challenge her intolerance of her romantic partners' foibles. In retrospect, Ellis believed that his own low frustration tolerance in the face of her resistance, combined with liking her too much "for her personal beauty and competence, and for her taking so readily to my theory and practice of REBT" (p. 1003), gave rise to the countertransference behavior of failing to challenge her. It also seems that what Ellis misses importantly is how he acted out his fear of the patient's criticalness toward the men with whom she was involved, including Ellis himself. In other words, Ellis probably felt what those men felt, and his fear of the patient's criticalness inhibited him from doing what he knew he should do. Then the patient was critical of him for his not doing that. Ellis's account is consistent with Coen's (2000) perception that therapists' difficulty tolerating their own uncomfortable affect inhibits patients' processing of emotions, and that therapists therefore need to continually work on expanding the range and intensity of emotions with which they are comfortable.

From a cognitive-behavioral perspective, countertransference can be viewed as the result of overgeneralized learning on the therapist's behalf. Just as transference can be considered a relationship template that patients apply to therapists (Gelso & Hayes, 1998), so too does the therapist perceive others, including patients, through a preformed set of lenses that are a byproduct of the therapist's learning history, culture, family of origin, and general life experiences. As a result of this very human state of affairs, the therapist may fail to discriminate properly between the patient and important others of whom the patient reminds the therapist (including the therapist!). J. L. Singer et al. (1989) posit that distorted information processing is a common countertransference manifestation, and therefore therapists must contend with a constant challenge to perceive patients as accurately as possible. Of course, this is no easy task. The key is to discern the similarities among and unique qualities in the patients that we see.

A classic study by Cutler (1958) supports the idea that countertransference can interfere with the therapist's information processing. Cutler studied the cases of two therapists' work with two patients. Before observing the cases, Cutler interviewed colleagues of the two therapists to ascertain areas of unresolved conflict in each therapist. In post-session interviews with the therapists, Cutler asked them what the patient had talked about during the preceding therapy hour. Cutler found that the therapists tended to either exaggerate or underestimate the frequency with which patients talked about material related to therapists' unresolved conflict. For example, if a therapist possessed unresolved issues related to his marriage and the patient discussed difficulties with her husband, the therapist tended to distort the frequency with which the patient talked about her marital problems. In another interesting study of therapists' distorted perceptions, McClure and Hodge (1987) found that therapists tended to misperceive patients as overly similar to themselves the more that they liked their patients. Conversely, the less therapists liked their patients, the more they tended to misperceive patients as overly dissimilar from themselves.

On a positive note, cognitive-behavioral theorists have offered valuable suggestions on how countertransference reactions may be clinically useful. For instance, countertransference reactions may be considered a "behavioral sample" of evidence for how the patient affects others (A. Beck, Rush, Shaw, Emery, 1979; J. Beck, 1996). This is similar to the notion in interpersonal theory that by allowing oneself to become "hooked" by the patient (i.e., to experience and observe one's reactions to a patient's interpersonal dynamics), the therapist gathers valuable information about reactions that others may experience when interacting with the patient. Finally, in terms of managing countertransference, Ellis (2001) suggests that therapists should allow themselves to be moderately biased and prejudicial but, consistent with the scientific tradition of the cognitive-behavioral approaches, should consistently test their ideas about patients.

Enhancing Cognitive-Behavioral Therapy Via Increased Attention to Countertransference

One of the hallmarks, and strengths, of cognitive-behavioral therapy has always been its scientific approach to treatment. Like scientists, cognitive-behavioral therapists formulate hypotheses about patients, gather and evaluate data, draw conclusions, and revise hypotheses based on the information they collect. In fact, therapists have a tremendous amount of information continuously available to them, both in the form of behavioral cues from the patient and, although typically downplayed in the cognitive-behavioral literature, internally from therapists themselves. As already discussed, some cognitive-behavioral theorists usefully view overt countertransference reactions as a behavioral sample of evidence about how the patient may influence others. However, it seems that more consideration needs to be devoted to the ways in which cognitive-behavioral therapists could benefit from attending to covert data—their perceptions, feelings, thoughts, attitudes, and visceral reactions. These sources of information are vitally important to psychoanalytic and humanistic approaches to treatment, as we discuss later in the chapter, but their role in cognitive-behavioral therapy is ambiguous. Judging from the relatively scant attention paid to the therapist's internal experience in the cognitive-behavioral literature, one might conclude that the therapist's use of this internal data is unimportant. On the other hand, we suspect that, in actuality, cognitive-behavioral therapists attend much more to their internal experiences than the professional literature would suggest.

Owing to their humanity, cognitive-behavioral therapists have a full range of inner experiences, and as a result, an enormous amount of internal data is constantly available to them. However, as any good scientist knows, data is valuable only to the extent that it is accurate, and the observed is affected by the observer. This is where countertransference enters the picture. Countertransference can influence a therapist to attend selectively to certain patient content and ignore other, more threatening material (Bandura, Lipsher, & Miller, 1960; Cutler, 1958). Countertransference also tends to distort one's perceptions, whether one is attending to information from within or without (McClure & Hodge, 1987). A cognitive-behavioral therapist and colleague of ours shared a story from his own background that illustrates the point.

The therapist had an initial session with a young woman who presented with poor self-esteem. The therapist had difficulty empathizing with the patient and her concerns. The patient was intelligent, socially skilled, and was succeeding in her career. Despite her many positive attributes, the patient tended to downplay them and did not take credit for her accomplishments. Like the patient, the therapist also was intelligent and interpersonally gifted, and he too also occasionally struggled with issues related to self-confidence and self-value. Due to both the patient's objective qualities and the therapist's unconscious attempt to distance himself psychologically from the patient, the therapist perceived the patient as a competent and capable person. In the initial session, he confronted her negative self-perception. He warmly, almost playfully, noted the lack of impartial support for her self-deprecating views, and he pointed to the abundance of evidence suggesting that a contrary self-image was not only defensible but warranted. The patient never returned for a second session.

At one level, the patient's premature termination could be viewed as the result of a technical mistake on the therapist's part; he confronted her too early in the work. At the same time, one wonders about the cause of the therapist's mistake. Working backward, the confrontation seems to have stemmed from an empathic failure that, in turn, was probably influenced by an unconscious and anxiety-producing overidentification with the patient. Of course, this sort of countertransference reaction can and does occur in all approaches to therapy. However, by downplaying the significance of the therapist's internal experience, cognitive-behavioral therapy may unintentionally promote countertransference behavior.

Despite the strides that have been made in cognitive-behavioral theory in attending to and conceptualizing countertransference, more work remains to be done. Foregoing radical changes to cognitive-behavioral theory, the therapist will never be as central a change agent as is the case in psychoanalytic and humanistic approaches. In these orientations, the therapist is more likely to use him or herself as a therapeutic tool, and thus the therapist's countertransference exerts a greater influence on the work.

PSYCHOANALYSIS: THE BIRTHPLACE OF COUNTERTRANSFERENCE REVISITED

When Freud first introduced the term countertransference in 1910, he [illegible]d great clinical significance to the construct. He wrote, "We have begun to consider the 'counter-transference,' which arises in the physician as a result of the patient's influence on his [the physician's] unconscious feelings, and have nearly come to the point of requiring the physician to recognize and overcome this countertransference in himself ... we have noticed that every analyst's achievement is limited by what his own complexes and resistances permit" (Freud, 1910/1959, pp. 144–145).

Given the importance Freud attached to countertransference in this quote, it is striking that he wrote so little subsequently about it. In his published writings, Freud mentions countertransference only four times. As discussed in chapter 1, Freud's seemingly contradictory emphases on therapists using themselves to understand patients and yet putting aside their own feelings while working with patients created a legacy of ambivalence toward countertransference. However, following several decades of relative neglect of the construct, the psychoanalytic community has devoted a tremendous amount of thought and energy to countertransference. Since the early 1950s, in particular, psychoanalytic theorists and clinicians have engaged in numerous and wide-ranging discussions on the various definitions, causes, manifestations, and effects of countertransference. Although the tide of popular opinion on these matters has ebbed and flowed in the past century, one constant is that countertransference is considered by psychoanalytic therapists to play a pivotal role in therapy, in terms of its potential for both interfering with and informing the work.

To be sure, the landscape within psychoanalysis has changed dramatically since its beginnings in Vienna, and so have views of countertransference within the analytic community. In short, "The days of viewing countertransference simply as a neurotic expression that needed to be resolved are essentially in the past" (Gelso & Hayes, 1998, p. 181). The prevailing contemporary view is that all therapists experience inner conflicts with virtually all patients, and when properly understood, these reactions can serve as a valuable source of information about treatment, about the patient, about the therapist, and about the therapy relationship (Gabbard, 2001; Weinshel & Renik, 1991).

Current psychoanalytic views of countertransference can be understood in terms of J. A. Hayes's (1995) structural theory that was discussed in chapter 2. Countertransference can be viewed as the result of unresolved conflicts within the therapist (i.e., countertransference *origins*) that are triggered by something the patient says or does (or doesn't say or do). In chapter 2, we referred to this as the *countertransference interaction hypothesis*. In other words, countertransference is not simply the result of the therapist's unresolved issues and it is never fully caused by the patient. If the former were true, all of our conflicts would be stimulated all of the time; clearly, and thankfully, this is not the case. Even chronic countertransference is not manifested all the time, in each moment of each session with each patient. If, on the other hand, countertransference were caused entirely by the patient, then all therapists would experience countertransference reactions in response to the same patient behaviors, but this is not the case either. One therapist may experience countertransferential rage toward a patient who is chronically late for appointments and another therapist's reactions may be free of countertransference. As noted in chapter 1, Gabbard's (2001) review of the contemporary psychoanalytic literature on countertransference points out that the prevailing view is that countertransference is co-constructed by therapist and patient. He writes,

> There is a movement in the direction of regarding countertransference as a *jointly created* phenomenon that involves contributions from both patient and clinician. The patient draws the therapist into playing a role that reflects the patient's internal world, but the specific dimensions of that role are colored by the therapist's own personality. (p. 984)

The notion that countertransference is co-constructed may be taken for granted by some therapists and theorists, especially those who share this view. However, it is worth pointing out that among ego psychologists, the prevailing view of countertransference is still closely aligned with Freud's classical definition. According to this perspective, countertransference is primarily a result of the therapist's unconscious conflicts. Whereas the therapist ideally is an empathic observer of the patient and her or his dynamics, countertransference reactions interfere with this empathic stance. In contrast to conceiving of the therapist as an observer of the patient, Sullivan (1954) asserted that the therapist was a participant observer in the therapy process. This "two person" view of therapy is consistent with recent developments emerging from the self-psychology perspective.

The self-psychology literature emphasizes an *intersubjective* perspective of countertransference (Stolorow, 1991; Stolorow, Brandchaft, & Atwood, 1987). Trop and Stolorow (1997) describe what is meant by this term. The intersubjective is "the field created by the interplay between the differently organized subjective worlds of patient and therapist" (p. 282). In other words, the subjective world of the therapist interacts with the subjective world of the patient and the end result cannot be understood without taking both worlds, and their interaction, into account. A molecule of water, for example, cannot be understood simply by knowing the properties of hydrogen, nor is knowledge of oxygen sufficient. One must understand the atomic structure of both hydrogen and oxygen and how they interact to comprehend why water is stable whereas the combination of one hydrogen atom and one oxygen atom is not.

Object relations theory has given rise to a relational conception of countertransference (Aron, 1991; J. R. Greenberg & Mitchell, 1983; Mitchell, 1988, 1997). This relational view is similar to the intersubjective perspective in that both emphasize the co-construction of countertransference. Object relations theorists emphasize the interactions between the patient's dynamics, including but not limited to transference, and the therapist's needs, conflicts, and vulnerabilities. Because patients may be attuned to and influenced by therapists' reactions, both countertransference-based and otherwise, an important aspect of this work is to explore patients' perceptions of the therapist.

Despite the movement within psychoanalytic thought toward a view of countertransference as co-constructed, there still exists within the literature what we believe to be excessive responsibility attributed to the patient for the therapist's internal and overt countertransference reactions. Klein (1946, 1975) cautioned long ago that the field might unwisely arrive at just such a position of attributing too much responsibility to patients for the therapist's countertransference. She foresaw the rise in popularity of the totalistic definition of countertransference as accountable for this state of affairs. Today, we find that ideas such as *projective identification* promote a dangerous abdication of responsibility for therapists' personal reactions to patients. In essence, projective identification posits that the therapist's feelings are the result of patient behaviors that reflect unconscious attempts to create in the therapist emotions that the patient finds intolerable (Ogden, 1994). Although patients may, in fact, try to stir particular emotions in therapists through a variety of means, we believe that it is imperative that therapists acknowledge their emotions as their own and take responsibility for them. Failure to do so increases the likelihood of countertransference acting out. The idea that therapists should take responsibility for their own feelings seems so commonsensical that it seems an almost unnecessary point of discussion (Eagle, 2000). Nonetheless, the literature on projective identification contains frequent warnings that the patient is not to be held responsible for the totality of the therapist's feelings (e.g., Spillius, 1992).

To be clear, and at the risk of redundancy, our view is that the therapist's conflicts are always implicated in his or her countertransference reactions. Whereas we tend to fundamentally agree with the view of countertransference as constructed by the therapist and the patient, the perilous underside to this conceptualization is that it runs the risk of minimizing the therapist's contributions and her or his responsibility for them. The historical view of the therapist as a blank screen, onto which the patient projects unconscious material for the therapist to analyze and interpret, still colors psychoanalytic thought and practice. To the extent that the emphasis on the patient negates an introspective stance by the therapist, the therapist may be at risk for acting on countertransference feelings. In addition, the therapist fails to avail him- or herself of potentially useful information. The movement from a one-person to a two-person psychology in most psychoanalytic circles has both positive and negative implications in terms of promoting the awareness and management of countertransference. On one hand, the two-person perspective recognizes the therapist's role as a participant observer who actively influences the therapeutic process in a variety of ways, including unconsciously. On the other hand, many proponents of the two-person psychology also espouse the concept of projective identification which, as we discussed in chapter 2, is often invoked in a way that minimizes the therapist's responsibility for her or his personal reactions to the patient.

In extreme instances, the therapist's unresolved conflicts can undermine and even dictate the course of therapy. Maroda (1991) describes this situation as "countertransference dominance" in which therapy is characterized "not by the patient's attempts to repeat the past, but by the analyst's" (p. 49). Maroda's (1991) description is akin to a repetition compulsion on the therapist's behalf in which the therapist unconsciously seeks to resolve an earlier conflict in her or his life. These conflicts may reflect both idiosyncratic and developmental difficulties. For example, according to Erikson, resolving developmentally normative conflicts (e.g., trust versus mistrust, intimacy versus isolation) is fundamental to psychological maturation. The less resolved a conflict is, whether it is idiosyncratic or developmentally based, the more likely that it will serve as a source of countertransference.

Countertransference Disclosures

Freud considered self-disclosure to be a mistake made by novice analysts in their attempts to help patients overcome resistance (Freud, 1910/1959). Freud thought such personal revelations were inappropriate, as they contradicted the principle that a therapist should act as an impenetrable mirror to a patient, reflecting only what is revealed by the patient. Jacobs (1997) noted that Freud's stance was likely influenced by the behavior of some pioneering analysts who disclosed their erotic feelings for patients, occasionally leading to sexually intimate relationships. Currently, according to research, psychoanalytic therapists are less disclosing than humanistic therapists, with cognitive-behavioral therapists seeming to fall somewhere between the two (Anderson & Mandell, 1989; Edwards & Murdock, 1994; Simon, 1988). On the other hand, theoretical and clinical literature reflects the fact that analytic therapists are more open to using self-disclosure than has been the case traditionally (Aron, 1996; Broucek & Ricci, 1998; Jacobs, 1999; Wilkinson & Gabbard, 1993). Although therapist self-disclosure is no longer considered off limits in the analytic community, there is general consensus that disclosures about one's countertransference reactions should be made sparingly and judiciously, if at all. The effect on the patient must be anticipated, and the therapist would do well to consider whether the intended consequences of the disclosure match the probable effects. For instance, whereas a therapist may intend to repair damage to the therapeutic relationship by making a countertransference disclosure, the patient may be left feeling unnecessarily burdened by the revelation with the end result being that the relationship is in no better shape than it was prior to the disclosure.

In conclusion, then, psychoanalytic conceptualizations of countertransference have shifted markedly from the days of Freud's initial use of the term. Early views of countertransference as an unhelpful byproduct of the therapist's neuroses now share the scene with conceptualizations of a phenomenon that is co-constructed by therapist and patient and that may be useful if attended to and managed properly. In addition, after languishing in relative neglect for several decades, interest in countertransference has increased greatly among psychoanalytic therapists.

HUMANISTIC–EXPERIENTIAL PERSPECTIVES ON COUNTERTRANSFERENCE

The two theoretical orientations that we have discussed so far, psychoanalytic and cognitive-behavioral, present contrasting views of the centrality of the therapist, as well as the therapist's countertransference, in treatment. Both the therapist and his or her countertransference are considered more important in psychoanalytic than cognitive-behavioral therapy. The humanistic and experiential approaches provide yet a third perspective. As is generally true of psychoanalytic theory, the therapist plays a crucial role in treatment, and the therapist's internal experience is a critical ingredient in the therapeutic mix. On the other hand, as is characteristic of the cognitive-behavioral realm, countertransference is discussed relatively infrequently in the humanistic literature. In part, the lack of attention to countertransference per se is more a matter of semantics than a reflection of the importance attached to the therapist's conflicts and vulnerabilities. Witness the following excerpt from Bugental (1978), in which he clearly discusses countertransference without naming it as such:

> The ideal psychotherapist is one who seeks to get and keep his or her act together. The ideal therapist recognizes that the emotions, conflicts, biases, and anxieties of the therapist's own life inevitably have their effects on the client's life, and this is not an idle recognition. Thus the ideal therapist accepts the responsibility for continuing self-monitoring to reduce the untoward impact of the therapist's distresses on the client. ... In short, though the therapist can never be expected to be "clear," without emotional or other hang-ups, the therapist most certainly can be expected to be one who makes more than usual efforts to be aware of and do something about those hang-ups. (p. 34)

Bugental goes on to write,

> Each therapist has a unique pattern of areas of open receptivity, areas of partial interference in which it is harder for the client's experiences to get through, and areas of relative or absolute blindness. ... Of course, I can't say with any surety what my own blind spots are for if I'm aware of them, they are no longer blind spots. ... In addition, with certain clients I will have particular patterns of positive and negative responses. As best I can, I try to keep aware of these, working out those that are chiefly from my own needs, while giving rein to those that seem to foster greater client inward searching. (pp. 43–44)

It is obvious that Bugental considers countertransference to be important, although as discussed previously with some cognitive-behavioral theorists (e.g., J. L. Singer et al., 1989), Bugental prefers to recast countertransference in language that is germane to his theoretical orientation. Doing so is neither unusual nor necessarily problematic. Mahrer (2001) put it this way: "In terms of vocabulary, I respect 'countertransference' as a psychoanalytic term; however, my vocabulary is experiential, not psychoanalytic" (p. 1021). Consequently, Mahrer discusses experiential "alternatives" to countertransference.

Beyond a semantic level, however, there is another reason why countertransference is not discussed as much in the humanistic literature as one might anticipate, given the importance that humanists attach to the therapist's subjective, inner world. One of the fundamental humanistic tenets is a belief in the inherent goodness of human beings.

The natural human tendency is believed to be toward health and development. By extension, one's inner experience largely is to be trusted (Tageson, 1982). This perspective stands in opposition to an emphasis on the therapist's negative qualities that are often associated with countertransference (e.g., unmet needs, biases, insecurities). Furthermore, from a humanistic vantage point, the therapist's thoughts and feelings are taken mostly as realistic, rather than as countertransference-based distortions. When the therapy relationship is characterized by genuine warmth and acceptance, according to humanists, countertransference recedes into the background. Countertransference is overshadowed by the therapist's authentic respect for and connection with the patient (Rogers, 1989).

According to Mahrer's (1986) experiential perspective, both the therapist and patient should be focused outwardly on some external "scene" characterized by the patient's strong affect. Countertransference is viewed as a distraction in that it directs the therapist's, and at times the patient's, attention toward the therapist rather than toward this external "scene." Thus, countertransference is seen as unhelpful rather than as a potentially useful source of information within this particular approach.

Countertransference as an Impediment

Countertransference also can pose an obstacle to the process and goals of person-centered therapy. Recalling Rogers's (1957) classic paper in which he outlined the necessary and sufficient conditions for therapeutic change, countertransference may serve as an impediment to the three therapist-offered conditions. To begin, countertransference may interfere with the therapist's authenticity or congruence, the first therapist-offered condition. When a therapist's conflicts, vulnerabilities, and insecurities are activated in session, the therapist who is aware of what is transpiring internally may feel enormous strain, especially when these states are "undesirable" ones. Countertransference feelings can run the gamut from rage to lust to despair to indifference. The person-centered ideal of congruence calls for therapists to behave in a manner that is consistent with their feelings. Clinical wisdom, however, would suggest otherwise when strong countertransference feelings are present. What, then, is a therapist to do? One of the keys to countertransference management is impulse control: maintaining the recognition that feelings are temporary, do not need to be acted upon, and may co-exist with other feelings that are obscured in the moment. To preserve a sense of authenticity or congruence when countertransference feelings run strong, then, may require therapists to stay true to their ideal therapeutic selves rather than to how they feel in the moment. That is, when acting on one's present feelings would put a therapist in a position of behaving incongruently with his or her therapeutic ideals, it is better to sacrifice the temporary congruence between one's feelings and actions in favor of the longer term congruence. A clinical example may help illustrate the point.

One of the authors was supervising a male therapist trainee who was working with a woman who had a history of severe abuse as a child and, in adulthood, a series of failed romantic relationships with men. Her pattern was to become sexually active very early in relationships with men as a means of trying to form secure attachments. At times, her sexual behavior was accompanied by displays of deep emotionality and self-disclosures that her partners considered inappropriate for the initial stages of a relationship. Her partners typically fled quickly under the weight of her need. Not surprisingly, early in the work, the patient engaged in highly erotic and seductive behavior with the therapist. She told the therapist that she fantasized about him, she provided graphic details of previous sexual encounters, and she asked the therapist what he thought of her outfits, which she indicated she had chosen with him in mind. In supervision, the therapist admitted to being attracted to and aroused by the patient, although he felt highly conflicted by these feelings. His conflicted feelings were tied up in his somewhat puritanical views on sexuality, and these countertransference feelings were amplified by his general discomfort discussing sex, because he had never deeply explored the attitudes that he had swallowed whole from his parents. He occasionally doubted his ability to manage his feelings of attraction toward his patient and often was unsure how to respond in session. Supervision was geared toward helping the therapist accept his feelings, discussing strategies for containing them, interpreting the patient's behavior, and preventing therapy from being undermined by the patient's behavior. During one particular therapy session, the patient began down a seductive path. She wondered aloud what the therapist looked like naked and asked if he was curious to know what she looked like underneath her clothes. Keeping his patient's best interests in mind and simultaneously maintaining his authenticity, the therapist replied by stating that he wanted to offer her a different relationship than she had experienced with other men and that she need not fear his abandonment. He gently explained that he would not answer her question any differently than that, as he believed it would take them away from the deeper work that needed to occur.

In this case, the therapist needed to come to terms with his attraction for the patient in order to get unstuck. Until that occurred, he felt somewhat paralyzed in session by the patient's sexualized behavior, fearing that he might both indulge it and reject her because of it. By accepting his feelings of attraction, the therapist was able to be more himself with the patient. Rogers (1989) goes so far as to say that therapists should be open to having their feelings known by the patient:

> The most basic learning for anyone who hopes to establish any kind of helping relationship is that it is safe to be transparently real. If in a given relationship I am reasonably congruent, if no feelings relevant to the relationship are hidden either to me or the other person, then I can be almost sure that the relationship will be a helpful one. One way of putting this that may seem strange to you is that if I can form a helping relationship to myself—if I can be sensitively aware of and acceptant toward my own feelings—then the likelihood is great that I can form a helping relationship toward another. (p. 51)

Like Rogers, other humanistically oriented theorists recommend open therapist disclosure as a means of facilitating genuine interpersonal relationships, although clinical discretion is always important (Curtis, 1981; Jourard, 1971). But to underscore our point, a therapist cannot simply be open without an associated risk of hurting the patient. Because the patient's best interests are a therapist's top priority, there are times when the therapist must sacrifice the openness dictate for a broader ideal that suggests that the therapist should be quiet when openness will hurt the patient.

In much the same way that countertransference can be an impediment to therapist congruence, it can also block unconditional regard for a patient. At their core, countertransference reactions are based on a perceived threat to the therapist, and it would be unusual to have unconditional regard for someone who represents a threat! On the contrary, when therapists' unresolved conflicts are provoked, therapists may resent patients for "putting them" in a difficult situation and may respond defensively, and even judgmentally.

Finally, in terms of condition set forth by Rogers (1957), the therapist's countertransference can hinder empathy. When one's conflicts or vulnerabilities are evoked, the natural human tendency is self-protective. When this occurs to a therapist, his or her attention is directed away from the patient, at least momentarily, toward some self-preserving element. As a result of this unconscious "turning inward," the empathic process is interrupted. It is possible, as we discuss in chapter 5, for therapists to subsequently use this turning inward to better understand patients, assuming that the therapist's conflicts and issues are sufficiently resolved. In other words, therapists can use their own past experiences of suffering to identify and empathize with the patient. A therapist must be careful, however, not to blur important distinctions that exist between self and other in the process. In fact, both over- and underidentification with the patient can result from countertransference, as was discussed in chapter 2. This idea shall be explored further in the following paragraph.

Empathy involves a partial or trial identification with the patient. However, at times the therapist will identify with the patient along dimensions that evoke the therapist's insecurities. For example, a therapist may recognize on some level that a patient's problem or personality or even physical features are similar to aspects of him or herself in ways that are conflictual and uncomfortable for the therapist. At these times, it is very difficult to maintain an appropriate therapeutic distance with patients. Research has demonstrated that countertransference is implicated in therapists' overinvolvement with patients, as well as with therapists' pulling away (Friedman & Gelso, 2000; Gelso et al., 1995, 1999; J. A. Hayes et al., 1998; Hill et al., 1996; Rosenberger & Hayes, 2002; Yulis & Kiesler, 1968). For some therapists, overidentification with patients may represent a type of countertransference-based ideal, one in which deep empathic attunement becomes confused with enmeshment. Therapists who lack sufficient self-differentiation may be especially prone to this "countertransference pitfall, wherein the therapist feels required to immerse himself or herself completely in the patient's experience, banishing his or her own psychological organization from the therapeutic dialogue so that he or she can gaze directly on the patient's subjective world with pure and pre-suppositionless eyes—surely an impossible feat for even the most gifted of therapists" (Trop & Stolorow, 1997, p. 282).

Like person-centered therapy, the process and goals of Gestalt and existential therapy can be obstructed by countertransference. For instance, countertransference is a potential block to the therapist's contact with the patient (Baehr, 2004). According to Yalom (2002), "The therapist's most important tool ... is his or her own person, through which the therapist engages with the patient" (p. 482). When countertransference interferes with the therapist's capacity to be him- or herself, authentic contact with the patient is difficult to sustain. Gestalt and existential approaches to therapy also emphasize the importance of awareness, both for the therapist in conducting therapy and as a desired outcome for the patient. However, countertransference often hinders the therapist's awareness, and in addition, research has suggested that therapist self-awareness is a critical component of countertransference management (J. A. Hayes, Gelso, Van Wagoner, & Diemer, 1991; Van Wagoner et al., 1991). Awareness in the therapeutic hour is especially compromised to the extent that the therapist's unresolved conflicts are unconscious. We believe that this is an aspect of countertransference to which humanistic therapists tend not to pay sufficient attention.

The emphasis on conscious awareness within humanistic theory, and the tendency to discount the effects of the unconscious, makes humanistic therapists particularly susceptible to not recognizing powerful influences on their behavior. We have witnessed a number of humanistic trainees get caught off guard by either their own or their patients' unconscious dynamics. Of course, we have seen the same thing happen to psychoanalytic trainees. The unconscious has a way of catching us all by surprise. Still, the humanistic tendency to attend to the here and now, to the contents of the conscious mind, fosters a certain vulnerability to the effects of the unconscious. Humanistic therapists would do well to stay open to and examine the possibility that unconscious factors are affecting their work with patients. Some humanistic therapists may disregard the effects of the unconscious because they reject traditional psychoanalytic conceptualizations of the unconscious. For these therapists, the model of the unconscious long ago proposed by Assagioli (1965) may prove more appealing. According to Assagioli, the unconscious comprises both lower and higher components. The lower unconscious most closely approximates Freud's concept of the unconscious. It is the seat of fundamental drives and primitive urges, typical kinds of dreams, obsessions, phobias, and emotionally charged complexes. The higher unconscious is the source of phenomena described by many humanists in volitional or teleological terms: altruistic love, artistic inspiration, heroic action, intellectual genius, illumination, and ecstasy. Because of its inclusion of the higher unconscious, Assagioli's (1965) theory may be more palatable to humanistic therapists than Freud's model. Because of Assagioli's emphasis on the lower unconscious as well, it should also prove useful in reminding humanistic therapists of the effects of their unconscious conflicts on their reactions to patients.

CONCLUSION

Sullivan (1954) once stated that we are all much more simply human than otherwise. This is true of therapists of all persuasions, and as a result of our humanity, we all experience countertransference and are affected by it in our work with patients. However, owing to differences in therapists' personal histories, the origins, triggers, and manifestations of countertransference are much more idiosyncratic than universal. Therapists need to recognize their own particular vulnerabilities and proclivities toward certain countertransference reactions. Furthermore, as discussed throughout the chapter, therapists of various theoretical persuasions may be susceptible to countertransference dangers in specific ways—cognitive-behavioral therapists may need to be more mindful of their covert reactions, psychoanalytic therapists must exercise caution not to attribute too much responsibility to patients for "causing" their countertransference, and humanists need to pay attention to the effects of the unconscious on their work. There is variable recognition across the three theoretical domains of what we consider to be fundamentally true: that countertransference is inevitable, important, and that it can affect therapy for better or for worse.

4

Countertransference and the Therapist's Experiential World

It is the thesis of this chapter, and in fact the entire book, that countertransference as we have defined it is best seen as residing within the broader context of the therapist's total experiential world as he or she conducts psychotherapy. This world may be variously labeled the *therapist's subjectivity*, *subjective experience*, *inner world*, or *experiential world*. We use these terms interchangeably throughout this chapter and book. Part of this inner world includes the therapist's internal reactions that are shaped by his or her past or present emotional conflicts and vulnerabilities, essentially our definition of countertransference, or at least the internal aspect of countertransference. But the therapist's inner world consists of much more than countertransference. It contains all the thoughts, images, affects, and even visceral sensations that the therapist possesses at any given time. This subjectivity exists in each and every psychotherapist in the interactions with each and every patient, regardless of theoretical orientation or approach. It exists even when treatment is manualized, when it is behaviorally oriented, and when it focuses on technique rather than relationship; and it plays an important, often vital, role in all psychotherapy and psychoanalysis.

In the present chapter, we focus on the therapist's experiential world. Although we do examine the countertransference portion of this world, our major emphasis in chapter 4 is on the inner world that is not countertransferential, as well as ways in which countertransference and noncountertransference-based inner experiences and outer reactions interact with one another.

When thinking of the therapist's subjectivity, one might be inclined to focus on the conscious experience of affects, images, and thoughts. However, it is important to understand that this subjectivity includes the full range of awareness or consciousness—from unconscious, to dim awareness, to full awareness on the part of the therapist. At the same time, it is our contention that the well-functioning therapist has greater access to inner experience, and at times to the full range of that experience. In other words, more of his or her inner experience is available to conscious awareness. In having this access, the therapist is able to be in touch with his or her experience and use it to better the treatment being offered. Again, this contention applies to all psychotherapies, the more technique-oriented and behavioral as well as the more dynamic and experientially oriented.

Much of the therapist's subjectivity, unlike the countertransferential portion, is conflict free. Thus, during the typical therapeutic hour, most of the time the well-functioning therapist does not experience emotional conflict, even when the inner experience has a negative valence. For example, a therapist may feel irritated or downright angry with his or her patient, or significant people in the patient's life, without this being conflictual for the therapist. That is, the feelings do not arise from the therapist's conflicts or vulnerabilities, and thus are not considered countertransferential. They may be natural, perhaps even inevitable, responses to the patient's verbal and nonverbal communication, responses that if not occurring would signify countertransference! For example, if the patient unfairly berates the therapist, it is not countertransferential for the therapist to feel annoyed or angry. At a more subtle level, in a subtle way, patients constantly stir certain internal reactions from their therapists, and many of these reactions are unpleasant or upsetting ones. We do not consider such reactions countertransferential unless they are rooted in the therapist's own conflicts and vulnerabilities. From a certain theoretical perspective (see Kiesler's, 2001, review, along with chap. 1, this volume), such natural feeling reactions are seen as *objective countertransference,* a term and concept that we believe contains considerable theoretical difficulties. We discuss so-called objective countertransference later in this chapter.

Perhaps the most fundamentally beneficial inner experience of the therapist is that of empathy. It is hard for us to imagine effective therapy in the absence of this quality (see Bohart, Elliott, Greenberg, & Watson, 2002, for ample empirical support). We do not think of empathy as a helping skill or an outer behavior, although it may, and usually does, show itself behaviorally. Instead, we think of empathy as an inner experience—a partial and temporary identification with the patient, in which the therapist for a period of time (varying from seconds to the entire hour) puts at least aspects of him or herself aside and dwells in the patient's inner world. As discussed many years ago by the psychoanalyst, Kris (1950), empathy requires that the therapist regress from the position of detached, intellectual observer to what Kris viewed as a more primitive kind of relationship in which the therapist temporarily becomes one with the patient. This requires a capacity for controlled and reversible regression. When the therapist either loses too much of the self for too long a period of time, or imposes her own issues into the identification, empathy slips over into countertransference. A clinical example of empathy that displays itself somatically and is not countertransferential is as follows:

> The therapist felt a knot in her throat that did not feel like her own affect. She asked the patient if what he experienced at the moment "was like a knot in his throat," and the patient said that was exactly what he was feeling. The client and therapist were able to explore the feeling and deepen the patient's experience of his feeling through tracking the somatic sensation and images that emerged. At one point in the session, the patient said that he could no longer feel the sensation, and that he felt confused and blamed himself for not being able to feel "right." At the same moment, the therapist noted a shift in her own body in which the knot in her throat changed to feeling like a heavy, dark cloud in her chest. The therapist (without reporting this new image) asked the patient if perhaps the sensation had shifted. The patient stopped for a moment to attend to himself, then reported that he was feeling a mysterious dark cloud in his chest that he did not know how to make sense of. Much of the remainder of the session was spent exploring the dark cloud in his chest and the feelings, images, and associations that emerged and connected back to painful experiences in childhood and to his sense of himself (Dr. Susan Woodhouse, personal communication, April, 2005).

We believe that the inner experience of empathy (and its outward expression) is an important ingredient in virtually all forms of psychotherapy. There is sound empirical evidence to support this assertion (see the Bohart et al., 2002, review).

A question may be raised about whether the therapist's own self is present or moved out of the experience during the process of empathic immersion. Kris's noted observation may seem to imply the latter, because he thinks of empathy as a process in which the therapist becomes one with the patient. Our view and experience suggest that the self of the therapist does not become eliminated or even put to the side. The self is always there, but aspects of the therapist's being are put to the side, for example, (a) the therapist's more self-centered needs, wishes, and fantasies; (b) the therapist's own issues and conflicts; and (c) the therapist's feelings about him or herself. With these moved to the side, so to speak, the therapist is better able to enter and dwell in the patient's world, tasting as if firsthand the patient's experience.

As the typical therapy hour unfolds, a number of elements are present. The therapist is about the business of trying to understand the patient and his or her problems and, at the same time, apply the techniques that emanate from the therapist's theory of therapy (whether the theory is formal or informal). Things usually unfold quickly and simultaneously during the hour, even in those "slow" hours in which not a lot seems to be happening. As the therapist listens, seeks to understand, and responds to the patient, the therapist's subjective world also unfolds. In other words, the therapist thinks, feels, experiences visceral reactions, and at times has images (i.e., imagines). These internal events, even when free of the therapist's personal conflicts and vulnerabilities, may vary on several interrelated dimensions. These include continua such as valence (positive vs. negative), intensity (high vs. low), clarity (vividly clear vs. dim and unclear), and state (relaxed vs. aroused). Where the therapist is at a given moment on these dimensions reveals much about the patient, as well as the therapist. We now describe these dimensions.

DIMENSIONS OF THE THERAPIST'S INNER EXPERIENCE

Valence

The valence dimension reflects the extent to which the therapist experiences positive or negative feelings, thoughts, visceral reactions, and/or images in the moment about the patient, and toward anything that is transpiring in the hour or even outside of the hour. The typical valence is most likely close to neutral, but on the positive side. Thus, as the therapist listens, seeks to understand the patient and the patient's experiences and affects, figures out what treatment options are most viable, and prepares for the next response, the valence in the therapist's subjective experience is close to neutral. At the same time, the abiding caring, concern, and wish to be helpful push the valence toward the positive side.

Positive feelings experienced in the hour include liking, a sense of empathic caring or concern, attraction of varying kinds, interest, and, more often than is apparent from the psychotherapy literature, a kind of nonsexualized loving. As we noted in chapter 2, loving feelings more likely occur in longer term treatments, where the participants get to know each other more deeply and fully as human beings. We noted the Greek word, *agape*, as reflecting this nonsexualized form of love. Another term that captures the affect we are describing is a deep kind of *prizing*, a term that was often used by Carl Rogers in discussions of his person-centered therapy. We view this prizing or loving as usually a very positive element of psychotherapy, and wonder about the efficacy of long-term treatments in which loving feelings are absent. Viewing these deeper forms of caring as countertransferential, to our minds, seriously misses the relational point of psychotherapy.

Negative affects, thoughts, visceral reactions, or images usually will revolve around some variant of sadness, anger, anxiety, or dislike (see the qualitative study of eight experienced therapists by J. A. Hayes et al., 1998). At times such affects stem from the therapist's countertransference (again, defined as reactions shaped by the therapist's emotional conflicts or vulnerabilities), whereas at other times, as we have said, negative reactions are not countertransferential at all. Instead, they represent healthy, expectable, appropriate, and fully human reactions to the patient and the material being presented. For example, the patient suffering from a narcissistic personality disorder during the course of treatment will inevitably elicit some negative internal reactions, even from the therapist who is a paragon of personal integration. When such a patient seems not to care at all for the person of the therapist, but instead values the therapist only to the extent that he or she can mirror the patient's greatness, this will pull for various negative internal reactions in the therapist. These are likely not countertransferential as we have defined this construct. However, if the therapist responds with excessive negative affect to this situation and acts these feelings out toward the patient, there certainly is a countertransference problem.

At times (e.g., when working with the narcissist, the sociopath, or the borderline patient), the absence of negative affect in the therapist will itself be a signal of a countertransference-based conflict. Negative subjective reactions also occur in response to people and experiences the patient is describing, especially those who have been psychologically damaging to the patient.

The therapist's internal reactions may be, and often are, mixed. For example, the therapist may experience positive feelings toward the patient, and negative thoughts and feelings toward persons the patient is describing from childhood who have caused emotional damage to the patient. This can also go the other way, where, for example, the therapist experiences positive reactions for a person who is behaving in a kindly way toward the patient, and negatively toward the patient for responding abusively toward that person. A case example from the first author's work demonstrates this:

> Rico, a 40-year-old geologist, had been in twice-a-week, analytically oriented psychotherapy with me for 7 months, and a significant part of the treatment focused on his yearning for a good relationship with a woman, while at the same time jumping from one relationship to another in an attempt to avoid facing his profound fears of being insufficient, weak, and deeply flawed as a man. He was insightfully exploring the many underlying issues involved in this theme when Rico became involved with a woman, Roberta, who seemed in most ways extremely well-suited to him. Roberta treated Rico with loving respect, and I found myself feeling appreciative toward her, admiring her insightful and caring way of being with Rico. I hoped he would be able gradually to come to grips with the profound conflicts he experienced around masculinity within the context of this good relationship. However, when Rico ended the relationship abruptly and painfully for Roberta, I felt sympathetic toward her and annoyed with Rico, even though I understood this as necessary defense at the time. He was just not ready for a healthy involvement then, but he was able to develop a very good relationship 2 years down the road.

The therapist of course may also experience mixed feelings toward the patient alone; for example, positive feelings toward the patient's courage and negative thoughts related to the patient's continued enactment of an entrenched pattern of behavior.

As we have implied, positive and negative internal reactions on the part of the therapist may or may not be countertransferential. The decisive factor is whether the reactions are influenced by the therapist's emotional conflicts and vulnerabilities. We have noticed a tendency among therapists to think of negative reactions as stemming from countertransference and positive reactions as being appropriate and not countertransference-based. This is very far from the truth, or at least our conception, as both positive and negative reactions in the therapist may or may not stem from countertransference. Whether or not they are countertransferential fundamentally depends upon the extent to which such reactions involve the therapist's own conflicts and vulnerabilities. Furthermore, as indicated in studies of countertransference behavior (Friedman & Gelso, 2000; Ligiero & Gelso, 2002), positive countertransference behaviors (e.g., befriending the patient, being oversupportive, agreeing too often) tend to block effective psychotherapy just as much as negative countertransference behavior.

Intensity

The therapist's inner experience will always vary in intensity, from very low to very high. Although it is tempting to conclude that very low intensity and very high intensity on the therapist's part are indicative of countertransference, we believe that such a conclusion misses the mark. The therapist may feel low-intensity reactions (e.g., boredom, low interest, emotional evenness, low engagement), and often does experience such reactions in the absence of countertransference. Low-intensity reactions are commonplace in work with patients who mute or repress their own affect. For example, the patient who speaks slowly, softly, and without affect is sooner or later going to stimulate a sense of tiredness, disengagement, or boredom in his or her therapist. Patients who mute affect tend to stimulate boredom or other low-intensity emotional reactions in their therapists, as well as in others in their lives. It is the therapist's job to help such patients work through the anxieties that are causing them to mute or repress their affect. Muted emotionality is especially common among patients with obsessive–compulsive personalities or personality disorders, as well as schizoid personalities. In both of these disorders, or styles, defenses against and muting of affect is a fundamental element of the psychopathology. Of course, the patient's cultural background must be carefully taken into account when making inferences about the meaning of what appears to be emotional inhibition. Cultures vary greatly on this dimension of expressiveness (McGoldrick, Giordeano, & Pearce, 1996).

Although the therapist's level of intensity is surely affected by the patient, it is also true that very low intensity on the part of the therapist often is indicative of countertransference. This is especially so when low intensity melds with indifference. The classical analyst, Greenson (1974), notes, for example, that the analyst cannot work well with a patient unless the analyst likes the analysand and is interested in him or her. For Greenson, indifference is a clear sign of countertransference. Such indifference, and low-intensity in general, certainly may signal a defense against painful or fearful feelings in the therapist.

Similarly, high intensity emotional reactions on the part of the therapist may or may not be indicative of countertransference. The idea that intense therapist reactions are an inevitable sign of countertransference issues results from both a misunderstanding of psychoanalysis and an accurate understanding of some psychoanalytic writings, especially classical theories that actually do imply that therapist intensity is problematic. Greenson (1974), for example, stated that all intense emotional reactions on the part of the therapist are suspect. Although we agree that this is often the case, we suggest that many intense reactions are not only nonconflict based, but also constructive and therapeutic. Our patients reveal the most painful, even horrific, experiences to us, and such experiences, in our view, often ought to stir our emotions, at times fairly intense emotions. The task for the therapist is far more complex than that implied by the classical analytic position as reflected in Greenson's views. From this classical perspective, the simple equation is that intense reactions equal countertransference. Intensity thus tells the therapist that there is a problem within him or her, and the therapist's task is to fix it, or at least not allow it to hinder the treatment.

From our perspective, emotional reactions that are anywhere on the continuum of intensity may or may not indicate countertransference. The therapist's daunting task is to gain understanding of his or her intense reactions, and to get a sense of what is causing them. It may indeed be that the patient's material is colliding with conflicts, vulnerabilities, and wounds within the therapist; or it may be that the patient's defenses are such that any sane therapist will react with intensity; or it may be that the patient's affects and experiences bespeak such suffering that they stir intense affects in the therapist. Although we believe that intense affect does not indicate countertransference in all cases, we do want to be clear that very high or low intensity of emotional reaction on the part of the therapist at least often suggests countertransference. It is a signal to the therapist to try to gain an understanding of where he or she is coming from.

Clarity

The therapist's inner experiences range from being very clear to very dim. Clear inner experiences are often vividly felt and visualized. The therapist's feelings toward the patient, for example, are within full awareness, and the therapist is able to have visual images related to these feelings. On the other end of the continuum, the therapist is unsure what he is feeling, even if his feelings are intense. An example of inner affect that is dimly experienced and unclear occurred early in the first author's career in his therapy with David, a 19-year-old university student. In this case, the reactions were both stimulated by the patient's needs and conflicts (mostly transference based) and rooted in the therapist's unresolved issues. Treatment occurred on a weekly basis over a period of 20 months. The case example is presented now in first-person terms:

> David was an emotional young client who yearned to be cared for. In a needy way, he pulled for loving and sympathetic feelings from others, even when feelings of love and sympathy were not experienced by others. He learned to be-

> have in relationships such that friends had to either come through with loving feelings, or feel guilty and bad for not caring enough. His friendships did not last long. Although these patterns were being explored over the course of many weeks and months, I did not see that they were invading the therapeutic relationship. This pattern was most notably enacted during one session in which the client asked me to hug him, and I did so, while at the same time experiencing discomfort and not experiencing feelings that were congruent with hugging another person. I should add that even in those days (the early 1970s), when physical touch was a more accepted part of treatment than it is today, especially within the humanistic therapies, I was never inclined toward physical touch in therapy. In any event, my feelings for and with this client were unclear to me, even though I was aware that I was feeling a lot (high intensity). However, things became very clear to me one night in the form of a dream. In the dream I had the client pinned to the ground and was choking him. And it felt good to be doing so. Needless to say, when I awoke, I was very unsettled. The realization came through very clearly that I was angry with this client, very angry. I had felt manipulated into caring for him over a period of many weeks. As this awareness emerged, I also became aware that on the mornings of our 9 a.m. sessions, I always seemed to feel grouchy, at times snapping at my wife and kids. As all of this became clear to me, I was able to modulate my feelings and reactions with David, and use them to communicate with David and better grasp his needs, the source of those needs, his relations with others, and others' reactions to him. My ability to modulate my feelings was aided by an understanding of my own personal conflicts around giving and receiving and a tendency toward guilt about not giving enough. These issues made me a fairly easy target for David's affective yearnings and his pull for affection. Although I never told David of my dream, the feelings that I came to grasp and understand in myself became an instrumental part of this successful therapy.

The moral of this story is that, as therapists, it is important that we bring dimly experienced feelings into awareness, that we make them clearer and more vivid, if we are to maximally help our patients. In the case example, the therapist's reactions were partly countertransference and partly noncountertransferential. The patient tended to manipulate others in order to get the nurturance he had lacked and desperately needed. The ways in which he required affection and nurturance would naturally create negative feelings in his therapist. However, the intensity of this therapist's reaction and the repression of negative affect reflect his own conflicts around giving, receiving, and guilt. This case example demonstrates how the therapist's noncountertransferential subjectivity may meld with countertransference or be invaded by it. The countertransference portion is also what caused him to dim his feelings in order to shield them from awareness.

State

Therapists' experience in the hour can vary from a deep kind of relaxation to a state of hyperarousal. The kind of relaxation to which we refer does not especially involve attention to the details of the patient's communication, but instead allows the therapist to pick up the less obvious communication, the more covert message from the patient. It is similar to Theodore Reik's famous concept of "listening with a third ear" and Freud's "even-hovering attention." Both concepts involve not listening to everything the patient says and not trying to make logical sense of the patient's communication. Both do involve a kind of relaxed state in which the therapist can take in the less rational and intellectual communication, the underlying message and music, so to speak. This state represents an inner experience that allows the therapist to come to understand aspects of the patient's inner world that are less obvious, more hidden. Of course, the therapist can also be so relaxed that he or she becomes inattentive to the patient and the patient's communication.

At the other end of this continuum, the therapist is in a state of hyperarousal, of attending to all aspects of the patient's communication. It is difficult to see how this state can be facilitative, at least for very long. Probably the most common state, as is the case with each of the dimensions we have described, is somewhere in the middle. The therapist is relaxed and attentive, but not highly so. Although this middle state is likely the most functional, there are surely times when the extremes, both that of relaxation and high arousal, yield the greatest insights and understandings.

A Postscript on Dimensions of Therapist's Inner Experience

In the practice of psychotherapy, it seems to be the case that therapists will not be especially aware of these four dimensions unless something is amiss. That is, each therapist probably has a place on each dimension where he or she resides, and it is only when there is a deviation from that personal norm that the therapist needs to pay attention. In other words, we therapists all probably have a circle of comfort on each dimension, and our alert signal goes up when we are moved out of that circle. It is important that we allow those signals and pay attention to them, for that is the first step toward understanding and using one's subjectivity to the benefit of the therapy. At the same time, it seems important that we each gain an understanding of our personal norms on each dimension, and do the necessary personal work if that place or circle is unhelpful or unhealthy. For example, a given therapist may be chronically on the negative (valence) and indifferent (intensity) side. This may reflect a chronic countertransference problem that calls for personal psychotherapy.

OBJECTIVE COUNTERTRANSFERENCE AND THE THERAPIST'S SUBJECTIVITY

The concept of objective countertransference appears to have been originated by the great psychoanalyst Donald Winnicott (1949) when he observed that there are feelings an analyst experiences that are warranted by the patient's behavior and personality. Winnicott thus defined *objective countertransference* as "the analyst's love and hate in reaction to the actual personality and behavior of the patient based on objective observation" (p. 195). The idea of objective countertransference (if not the term itself) may be seen in the currently popular belief within some relational, interpersonal, and intersubjective psychoanalytic theories that many therapist reactions to patients are fully determined by patients' pathology, transference, and defenses. As previously noted, writing about projective identification at times has this flavor (Eagle, 2000; Gabbard, 2001).

The concept of objective countertransference is most clearly seen in the writing of the interpersonalist, Donald Kiesler (1996, 2001). For Kiesler (2001), objective countertransference "refers to the constricted feelings, attitudes, and reactions of a therapist that are evoked primarily by the client's maladaptive behavior and that are generalizable to other therapists and to other significant persons in the client's life" (p. 1057). In his interpersonal communication therapy, Kiesler employs the concept of *complementarity* to get at this objective countertransference. Complementarity refers to the interpersonal response that the patient "pulls" from the therapist, as well as virtually any significant others in the patient's life.

When the term *objective countertransference* is used, it is juxtaposed to a partner term, *subjective countertransference*. This latter term is used to indicate the therapist's response that is determined by his or her own conflicts and problems. It has been our contention that the differentiation of countertransference into objective and subjective is not the most fruitful, scientifically or clinically. First, such a distinction implies that virtually all therapist reactions are countertransferential. Second, this distinction often misses the fact that what may seem like objective countertransference is very often fundamentally rooted in the therapist's conflicts and vulnerabilities. In other words, even when it is not obvious, a "hook" usually resides within the therapist that connects to the patient's "pulls." The concept of objective countertransference makes it too easy to ignore that hook, especially when in a certain way we therapists would be relieved not to have any hooks (i.e., unresolved problems spilling into the work). In essence, the second reason why the objective–subjective countertransference distinction is not very sound is that, upon close inspection, most cases that look like objective countertransference involve a therapist whose conflicts and vulnerabilities are implicated, to one degree or another, in the reactions.

A third problem with the objective–subjective distinction is that it implies that a cluster of the therapist's subjective reactions are objective. To the contrary, the inner experience of the therapist is never objective, that is, free of personal feelings. The therapist's inner experiences are overwhelmingly subjective, and in this sense the concept of objective countertransference represents a contradiction in terms.

Finally, division of therapists' reactions into objective and subjective countertransference misses the fact that some therapist reactions are normal and healthy reactions to patient expressions that are themselves normal and healthy. As therapists, we have many appropriate internal responses to patients' appropriate and desirable feelings and behaviors. Such therapist responses are an extremely important part of psychotherapy, and they must not be excluded from our conceptualizations through a view that all therapist reactions are either objective or subjective countertransference.

To be sure, we would offer that in all therapy relationships, the patient exhibits a press or a pressure on the therapist to feel, think, and behave in a certain way. This press may come from the patient's transference, nontransference defenses, or personality needs and structure. For the therapist to feel or experience what is evoked from the patient is best viewed as simply the therapist's affect or cognition, or perhaps patient-evoked affect and/or cognition. It need not be given surplus meaning by calling it countertransference.

THE ROLE OF THE THERAPIST'S SUBJECTIVITY

The role of the therapist's inner world, if not the nature of that world, will be strongly influenced by therapist's theoretical allegiance. In general, the therapist's emotional reactions are viewed as less significant in the behaviorally oriented therapies, and as more significant in psychodynamic and humanistic-experiential therapies.

The Therapist's Subjectivity in Behavior Therapy

In considering the significance of the therapeutic relationship in contrast to technique in cognitive and behavioral therapies, we (Gelso & Hayes, 1998) earlier presented the following analogy:

> The second author recently had a house painted. His relationship with the painter, while cordial, was fairly unimportant in determining the appearance of the house when the painter was finished. The final product was largely a function of the painter's skill and effort. The same author also has been seeing a chiropractor for several weeks. Whereas the painter applied the tools of her trade to an inanimate object with which she had no relationship (at least as we would define it), the chiropractor has been executing his skills on a live human being who has not only lower back pain, but also a mix of apprehension, curiosity, and reserved optimism. Because the second author is the direct recipient of the chiropractor's interventions, his relationship with the chiropractor is of somewhat greater consequence than his relationship with the painter. After all, it requires considerable faith on a patient's part to allow another individual to manipulate one's body in such a way that fairly loud and peculiar noises emanate from one's vertebrae. Additionally, and more seriously, a patient's confidence in a chiropractor affects the patient's regimen prescribed by the chiropractor. However, given that the chiropractor is directly treating the patient's back, not the patient's thoughts or desires or values or emotions, it seems reasonable to conclude that a successful outcome will largely be dictated by the efficacy of the chiropractor's techniques and not the quality of the patient–chiropractor relationship. ... Cognitive-behavioral therapists generally would agree that the client–therapist relationship is of greater significance than the patient–chiropractor relationship, but not by much. (pp. 191–192)

Just as the relationship has played second fiddle to techniques in cognitive-behavior therapies, the therapist's inner world has not been seen as especially important. However, as behavior therapists have increasingly paid attention to the therapeutic relationship (Goldfried & Davila, 2005; Holtforth & Castonguay, 2005; Lejuez, Hopko, Levine, Gholkar, & Collins, 2005), so too have they gradually incorporated the therapist's inner world among their list of important therapeutic constructs. Several contemporary cognitive-behavioral therapies view the therapeutic relationship and the therapist's feelings toward the patient (including countertransference) as very significant (e.g., S. C. Hayes, Strosahl, & Wilson, 1999; Kohlenberg & Tsai, 1995; Linehan, 1993). For example, in S. C. Hayes et al.'s (1999) acceptance and commitment therapy (ACT), the therapist is expected to be open, accepting, respectful, and loving toward the patient. Further when "Acceptance and Commitment Therapy is done properly, relationships are intense, personal, and meaningful" (p. 280). Thus, the therapist is not only expected to feel a lot and show his or her feelings, but the therapist's feelings are a fundamentally important part of therapy.

Similarly, in Marsha Linehan's dialectical behavior therapy (DBT), a behavioral treatment that has been especially developed for patients suffering with borderline personality disorders, the therapist's affective world is vital, at times even lifesaving. Witness Linehan's (1993) comment on what she refers to as relationship acceptance:

> In relationship acceptance the therapist recognizes, accepts, and validates both the patient and himself or herself as a therapist with this patient as well as the quality of the patient–therapist relationship. Each is accepted *as it is* in the current moment; this includes an explicit acceptance of the stage of therapeutic progress or lack thereof. Relationship acceptance, like all other acceptance strategies, cannot be approached as a technique for change—acceptance in order to get past a particular point. Relationship acceptance requires many things, but most importantly it requires a willingness to enter into a situation and a life filled with pain, to suffer along with the patient, and to refrain from manipulating the moment to stop the pain. Many therapists are not prepared for the pain they will encounter in treating borderline patients, or for the professional risks, personal doubts, and traumatic moments they will encounter. The old saying "If you cannot stand the heat, don't go into the kitchen" is nowhere more true than in working with suicidal and borderline patients. (pp. 515–516)

In both ACT and DBT, what the therapist feels and thinks is extremely important to the work. For Hayes and his ACT collaborators, a premium is placed on experiencing and communicating positive feelings. Perhaps because Linehan is focusing on the treatment of profoundly troubled patients, she also emphasizes importance of the therapist being a genuine human being, who accepts and even experiences the patient's great pain, and does not try to manipulate the patient into feeling differently. Although the relationship and the therapist's feelings are used in DBT, in part to facilitate the patient's following the treatment regimen, they are also in part seen as curative in and of themselves.

So the world of behavior therapy has changed a great deal in the greater than half century of its existence as a formal treatment approach, and arguably the greatest change has been in the realm of the therapeutic relationship and the therapist's inner experience. Still, with some notable exceptions, this inner experience is not as central as it is in the analytic and humanistic therapies.

The Inner World of the Psychoanalytic Therapist

In virtually all psychoanalytic therapies, the therapist's inner world is vitally important. However, the way in which it is important depends upon which analytic theory is being addressed. Pine (1990) divided the world of psychoanalytic theory into four clusters or psychologies: drive psychology, ego psychology, object relations theory, and self-psychology. Each theory contains a somewhat different emphasis in terms of personality development, psychopathology and health, and treatment. As far as the inner world of the therapist, the four clusters can readily be combined into two: classical theory (drive and ego psychology) and two-person theories (object relations and self-psychology, including the latter's intersubjective extension).

Like cognitive-behavior therapy, the world of psychoanalysis has changed substantially over the decades since its inception. This change is especially marked in the area of the analyst's inner experience. As for the beginnings, we take Freud's (1912/1959a) famous Surgeon's Quote as the starting point: "I cannot recommend my colleagues emphatically enough to take as a model in psycho-analytic treatment the surgeon who puts aside all his own feelings, including that of human sympathy, and concentrates his mind on one single purpose, that of performing the operation as skillfully as possible" (p. 327). Freud did not mean that the therapist should have an internal world devoid of content. However, the content involved thoughts and fantasies aimed at understanding the patient, and a kind of openness or receptivity (fostered by evenly suspended attention) that allowed the therapist to perceive and subceive material that was not conscious in the patient. The focus was to be on the patient, as well as the therapist's thoughts, associations, and fantasies about the patient and the patient's material. The therapist was not supposed to feel a lot, and strong or intense feelings were especially eschewed. After all, these would do the surgeon no good, and if the surgeon experienced them, they likely had their basis in the surgeon's unresolved complexes and conflicts.

Over the years, there has been a liberalization of thought within psychoanalysis regarding what the analyst and/or therapist could and should experience. The 1950s were signal years for this liberalization. For example, a paper by Crowley (1950), interestingly titled "Human Reactions of Analysts to Patients," pointed out that noncountertransference reactions of analysts not only could not be avoided, but could be tremendously helpful to analysis. Crowley lamented that the analyst's appropriate, nonexaggerated, and nonanxious reactions to the patient were much neglected in the analytic literature, and their significance was belittled. He believed that analysis could be done successfully in no other way than by use of the analyst's own personal reactions to the material. Otherwise, the analyst's comments and interpretations are "bound to be mediocre" (p. 87).

The interpersonal and now the relational branches of psychoanalysis have always emphasized the vital importance of the analyst and/or therapist making use of the full range of his or her feelings to understand and help the patient. Sullivan certainly emphasized this (see Evans's, 1996, analysis of Sullivan's conceptions), and for interpersonal analysts such as Clara Thompson (1956), the therapist's total personality, which was mostly healthy and nonconflicted, was a vital part of successful treatment. Further, she noted that we therapists need to relate to patients with more than our intellects, that we often feel things that do not reach conscious awareness. For example, Thompson (1956) asks, "... why do I frequently yawn with a certain patient, why do I feel restless with another, and vaguely annoyed at times with a third? Is it simply the time of day or my state of weariness, or is it some more serious failure of communication?" (p. 356).

Thompson, like so many analytic and nonanalytic writers, also underscores that the internal state of goodwill and genuine concern is vital to the work. Many point to the necessity of interest, caring, liking, and other positive reactions.

The attention to the analytic therapist's internal world has certainly been evident in the analytic literature from the 1950s on. In fact, in 1956, Thompson wondered if analytic authors had gone too far in their emphasis on such phenomena. However, it appears that there has been a steady increase in attention to this internal world, both countertransference and noncountertransference. Presently, this emphasis is most clearly evidenced in the works of relational and intersubjective psychoanalysts (see Mitchell & Aron, 1999), who view themselves a adhering to two-person psychologies rather than one-person psychologies that they attribute to their more classical counterparts. A core element in this two-person conception is that the patient and therapist together create whatever happens in the therapy, including the patient's unfolding material and the therapist's subjective and external reactions. As for the therapist's internal world or subjectivity, Renik (1993), for example, addresses the topic forcefully when he tells us "It seems to me pointless to ask an analyst to set aside personal values and views of reality when listening or interpreting. Everything an analyst does in the analytic situation is based upon his or her personal psychology. This limitation cannot be reduced, let alone done away with; we have only the choice of admitting it or denying it" (p. 559). The analyst "cannot eliminate, or even diminish, his or her subjectivity. However, an analyst can acknowledge his or her irreducible subjectivity and study its effects" (p. 560). Thus, our feelings and subjectivity must be acknowledged and experienced. This subjectivity enters into every single thing we do with our patients, and it also inevitably affects and is affected by the patient. It is stirred by the patient's offerings, just as it affects those offerings. We need to examine the effects of and upon our subjectivity in the hour.

Although certainly not all analysts accept this relational perspective, the field has moved very far away from the attitude reflected in Freud's surgeon's analogy. For virtually all psychoanalysts and analytic therapists, the inner world of the therapist is a key element of psychotherapy and psychoanalysis, and this inner world includes subjective experience that is relatively free of the therapist's unresolved conflicts and vulnerabilities as well as subjective experience that is embedded in them.

The Inner Experience of the Humanistic Therapist

Unlike the two general theoretical systems we have discussed, the humanistic practitioners and theoreticians have viewed the inner world of the therapist as tremendously important and of great potential benefit from the very beginnings of this general theoretical system. To understand the humanist's view of the inner world of the therapist, it is helpful to divide humanistic and/or experiential therapy into its two primary approaches, person-centered therapy and gestalt therapy. Each of these approaches is also evidenced in what has come to be called process-experiential (L. S. Greenberg, Rice, & Elliott, 1993) or emotion-focused (L. S. Greenberg, 2002) therapy, to be discussed. We should note that psychotherapies labeled as *existential* may also be placed under the general humanistic umbrella, especially regarding their views of the role and relevance of the therapist's inner experience in therapy.

For Carl Rogers and his client-centered and later person-centered therapy, effective counseling and psychotherapy involved certain therapist attitudes: (a) empathic understanding of the client, (b) unconditional positive regard for the client, and (c) what was termed congruence within the therapist. These attitudes were a key part of what Rogers termed the necessary and sufficient conditions for successful therapy (Rogers, 1957). These conditions are, to a very important extent, part of the therapist's internal world, although of course the conditions must be communicated to the client in one way or another. In brief, the therapist must climb into the client's world, putting himself or herself aside temporarily, and experience during the hour what it is like to be the client (empathic understanding). In effective therapy, also, the therapist prizes the client, experiences warmth and positive regard for the fundamental person of the client, without conditions (unconditional positive regard). Finally, the therapist must be at one with himself or herself, in touch with his or her inner experiencing, and not hide who he or she is (congruence). That is, the therapists must not deny, but instead be fully aware of their inner experience with the client and be able to show their personhood to the client. For example, in his famous filmed therapy session with Gloria, Rogers comments after the therapy session that he would like his clients to "see all the way through me." Obviously, the three conditions are not only internal states or attitudes, but the must be conveyed to the client if therapy is to be successful.

The connection of Rogers' concept of *empathy* to countertransference is clearly depicted in one of Rogers's (1951) early writings when he says "In a therapeutic relationship where the therapist endeavors to keep himself out, as a separate person, and where his whole endeavor is to understand the other so completely that he becomes almost an alter ego of the client, personal distortions and maladjustments are much less likely to occur" (p. 42). In this way, the therapist's ongoing effort to enter into the client's inner world empathically precludes or at least substantially reduces the likelihood of countertransference reactions. We should note, however, that as Rogers continued to develop his theory, he placed greater emphasis on the therapist putting himself or herself into the relationship, rather than staying out, while at the same time maintaining the importance of ongoing and deep empathic immersion (Gelso & Hayes, 1998). The therapist's empathic immersion is beautifully described by Rogers (1951) in the introduction to what is perhaps his most influential work, as follows:

> This book is about the highly personal experiences of each one of us [clients and therapists being studied]. It is about a client in my office who sits there by the corner of the desk, struggling to be himself, yet deathly afraid of being himself—striving to see his experience as it is, wanting to *be* that experience, and yet deeply fearful of the prospect. This book is about me, as I sit there with that client, facing him, participating in that struggle as deeply and sensitively as I am able. It is about me as I try to perceive his experience, and the meaning and the feeling and the taste and the flavor that it has for him. It is about me as I bemoan my very human fallibility in understanding that client, and the occasional failures to see life as it appears to him, failures which fall like heavy objects across the intricate, delicate web of growth which is taking place. (p. x)

For the gestalt therapist (e.g., Yontef, 1993), a great emphasis is also placed on the therapist's awareness of his or her internal experiences at the moment, and, to an extent that is greater than in person-centered therapy, there is a focus on the use of these experiences to spontaneously derive responses to the client. The therapist's responses may be in the form of sharing with the client what the therapist is feeling, or they may involve the use of gestalt techniques aimed at helping the client experience in the here and how, and thus become emotionally aware if his or her inner workings.

For the humanistic therapist, the cognitive part of the therapist's inner world is deemphasized. The feeling or emotional aspect of the therapist's experience is what is most central, and the intellect, more than anything, may get in the way of a constructive process. In fact, Fritz Perls, the founder of gestalt therapy, often belittled the intellectual side of the therapist's experience, likening it to mind fucking in his colorful parlance (Perls, 1969).

All present-day integrations of person-centered and gestalt therapy have this great emphasis on the therapist being in touch with his or her inner experience, being emotionally present in the moment, being internally congruent, and being genuine with the client in a way that is constructive. Emotional spontaneity is also a key element, although virtually all of the current humanists underscore that this spontaneity is very different from saying whatever one feels. It is a controlled spontaneity in which the therapist's countertransference conflicts are held at bay and feelings are shared with the intent of fostering awareness and growth. This sharing is to be done in the context of empathic concern for the client, which is always at center stage (see Bohart, 2003; L. S. Greenberg, 2002). In these therapies, it is vital that the therapist be in touch with his or her negative feelings and use these feelings for the client's benefit. As L. S. Greenberg (2002) states, "Anger expressed as attack, or a bored feeling expressed as withdrawal, are not facilitative, whereas using these as information on which the therapist can reflect, and disclosing them to the client as information to be explored, when appropriate, can be helpful" (p. 75).

THE THERAPIST'S SUBJECTIVITY: A TRANSTHEORETICAL APPROACH

We have seen that the therapist's internal countertransference is embedded in the larger world of the therapist's inner experience or subjectivity. This broader world is a vital part of all psychotherapy, and the therapist's inattention to his or her own subjectivity when doing therapy will surely reduce effectiveness or even yield ineffectiveness. This assertion applies most clearly to the part of the therapist's subjectivity that we call countertransference (see empirical review by Gelso & Hayes, 2002). However, it also applies to the portion of the therapist's inner experience that is not driven by countertransference.

As we have suggested, the major theoretical clusters all now subscribe to the idea that the therapist's inner experience is an important part of treatment success. To be sure, there are clear differences in the extent to which cognitive-behavioral, psychoanalytic-psychodynamic, and humanistic-experiential therapies emphasize the therapist's inner experience as an ingredient of effective treatment. The humanistic and dynamic therapies place the therapist's subjectivity at center stage more than does CBT (cognitive-behavioral therapy). For many currently popular cognitive-behavioral approaches, it is important that the therapist has and expresses positive feelings toward the patient, whereas the other two major systems emphasize that it is crucial for the therapist to be aware of all kinds of inner experiences, including negative ones. There are also differences in just how this inner experience works and ought to work within the three clusters. But make no mistake, virtually all of the modern and major systems do subscribe to the importance of what the therapist feels, thinks, fantasizes, and viscerally experiences in the psychotherapy hour.

Although we have asserted that all therapists need to be in touch with their inner workings, regardless of theoretical orientation, not all therapists need to attend to their subjectivity to the same degree or in the same way in order for the treatment to be effective. The degree and manner are deeply linked to the therapist's theory. For example, the CBT therapist does not need to be attentive to his or her subjectivity to the same extent or in the same way as dynamic and humanistic therapists. That is because the CBT therapist devotes much more of his or her energy to figuring out the parameters of the patient's problems, and to the formulation and implementation of treatment techniques that help solve those problems. The inner experience that is focused on is also more in the cognitive realm that in other theories. For the most part, this is perfectly fine; and there is certainly an enormous amount of empirical support for the effectiveness of CBT on the whole (Lambert & Ogles, 2004). At the same time, most current CBT theoreticians and therapists would agree that it is important that the therapist experience positive feelings and attitudes toward the patient (liking, respect, caring, etc.) and communicate these to the patient in ways that are consistent with the CBT approach.

In addition to experiencing and communicating positive feelings, more than may be typically acknowledged in CBT, it is important that the CBT therapist be in touch with negative feelings and thoughts. Even when such feelings and thoughts are not rooted in the therapist's inner conflicts and vulnerabilities (countertransference), they need to be paid attention to. This is so because such inner experiences can have a tremendous, if subtle, effect on the selection and implementation of techniques; and of course negative feelings will often come across to patients, especially if therapists are unaware of these feelings. We suspect that therapists' unacknowledged and unmanaged feelings and thoughts, whether countertransferential or not, are the source of a high percentage of treatment casualties in CBT, as well as in other approaches. This problem is most likely to occur when the feelings and thoughts are negative, but the effects may be equally damaging when feelings are too positive. Excessively positive feelings, as we have discussed, are very likely to be tied to the therapist's countertransference problems.

We have been focusing mostly on the therapist's inner experience and the importance of therapist self-awareness. Much less has been said about the value of direct expression of the therapist's feelings toward the patient. Although it seems clear that well-timed and judicious self-disclosures on the part of the therapist can be quite helpful under certain conditions (see Hill & Knox's, 2002, thorough summary of research findings), the value of therapists' sharing their thoughts and feelings will depend, to a great extent, on the theoretical framework in which such sharing is done. Thus, for example, the classical psychoanalytic therapists who care deeply about their patients, who implement their theory effectively, and who believe that self-disclosure typically will hinder the analytic process (and thus rarely disclose) are likely as effective as gestalt therapists who care deeply about their clients, who implement their theory effectively, and who believe that being spontaneous and wisely sharing feelings is the best way to proceed (and thus often disclose). In sum, although there is a world of clinical evidence, as well as emerging empirical evidence, to indicate that it is important, perhaps vital, for therapists to be in touch with their inner world, whether countertransference based or noncountertransferential, just how and how much of that world should be expressed during the hour, and in which ways this inner world should be expressed, are another matter, one that is deeply bound to the therapist's vision of psychotherapy and interpersonal relationships. It is very doubtful that there is a right amount or a right way that cuts across theories, or individual therapist preferences and patient needs for that matter.

Finally, a distinction must be made between direct verbal expression of feelings and indirect expression. Direct self-disclosures as are typically written about in the psychotherapy literature (Hill & Knox, 2002) are of the first kind. Indirect expression, however, involves the multitude of nonverbal expressions on the part of the therapist, as well as the overall ambience that the therapist helps create in the hour. It is this indirect expression that we believe must be largely positive if the treatment is to be successful (see Lambert & Barley's, 2002, review of empirical findings, which we believe strongly supports this assertion). In other words, therapists show in a multitude of ways what they feel toward their patients; and a therapeutic ambience that embodies such positive therapist feelings as empathy, positive regard, respect, liking, and prizing of the patient goes a long way toward effective psychotherapy.

CONCLUSION

The inner experience of the psychotherapist during the treatment process includes countertransference, but involves much more than countertransference. In this chapter, the focus has been on the noncountertransference portion of the therapist's subjectivity, which is the most commonly experienced part. Like countertransference, the noncountertransference experience of the therapist can be for better or worse, and the goal of practitioners and researchers alike must be to understand how to use the therapist's inner experience for the betterment of psychotherapy. Much has been done in this area. For example, the decades of research on therapist empathy as an internal experience, as well as an enactment of that experience, has left little if any doubt that this element of treatment is of great significance. It helps the patient when present, and does not help but instead may harm the patient when it does not exist or exists in very low amounts. Other internal experiences of the therapist have been much less studied, and some, for example, loving feelings, have been avoided. Although therapists of different theoretical orientations do not need to devote themselves equally to the understanding of their subjectivity, all need to devote some energy to this, and to the use of that subjectivity for the betterment of the patient and the work.

5

The Management of Countertransference

Given the pervasive and inevitable nature of countertransference, an important question arises as to how to manage it. For the sake of clarity, it is important to be explicit about what we mean by countertransference "management." To the extent that something interferes with the process of therapy or the attainment of therapeutic goals, that thing—whatever it is—needs to be controlled or regulated as best one is able. On the other hand, if something has the potential to facilitate the process and enhance the outcome of therapy, one should judiciously cultivate it and use it as an ally in one's clinical work. This, in essence, is what we mean by managing countertransference. Consistent with the view of countertransference as a "double helix" (Epstein & Feiner, 1979), with its prospective vices and virtues intertwined, successful countertransference management requires that therapists be alert both to acting out in detrimental, unintended ways and to acquiring clinically significant insights as a result of their reactions to patients.

The question of how to manage countertransference might best be considered as three separate questions. First, how can the negative effects of countertransference be prevented or at least made less likely to occur? Second, after countertransference has negatively affected the work, how might one repair the damage and minimize its adverse impact? Third, from a more positive vantage point, how can therapists use countertransference to benefit their work with patients? We address these questions sequentially in this chapter, and in doing so, we discuss theory, research, and clinical material related to the management of countertransference.

PREVENTING ADVERSE EFFECTS FROM COUNTERTRANSFERENCE

Let us take up the first question: What can help prevent the negative consequences of countertransference from occurring? To avoid countertransference reactions altogether, a therapist probably has but two options: Transcend the human condition or stop seeing patients. Although these options, of course, are somewhere between implausible and preposterous, they nevertheless may be instructional. For instance, regarding the human condition, it is probably not difficult to call to mind colleagues who seem to believe that they have risen above it all. They perceive themselves to be self-actualized; we may perceive them to be remarkably lacking in self-awareness. They don't consider their work to be affected by countertransference; we imagine their work to be riddled with it. Fortunately, in our experience, these therapists are rather rare, although their potential effects on patients, co-workers, and the public's perception of psychotherapy can be great.

It is also worth noting that the other alternative to avoiding countertransference, not seeing patients, occasionally is a painful reality faced by therapists and trainees. This can take on a limited scope, as in not seeing specific kinds of patients. The second author, for example, engaged in a nongraceful, somewhat hostile confrontation early in therapy with a patient who resembled his [the therapist's] father in unsettling ways. The patient, who was very much in need of help with relational and occupational issues, never returned. Thereafter, the second author decided not to work with patients who shared this patient's, and his father's, particular feature until he had sufficiently resolved the basis for his countertransference reaction.

The decision not to work with patients is sometimes involuntary, however, and of a broader scope. For instance, countertransference issues may be at the heart of unethical behavior that results in therapists having their licenses suspended or revoked, and infrequently, chronic countertransference problems have necessitated that therapists in training pursue alternative careers. From our experience, these situations with trainees are extraordinarily painful for everyone involved: the student, clinical supervisors, program faculty, and the trainee's classmates, family, and friends. Faculty who take seriously their responsibilities as gatekeepers to the profession will, on occasion, face decisions in which they must determine if a student's countertransference issues are so severe that they call into question the student's fundamental ability to practice psychotherapy. Such questions create a domino effect: If the answer is yes, then what can be done to help the student? What is the likelihood that various interventions will help resolve the problematic countertransference issues? If the intervention involves personal therapy for the student, how will confidentiality issues be handled? To illustrate, one of the authors supervised an otherwise promising student whose anxiety with patients was so extreme that he engaged in what could best be described as socially repulsive behaviors. When these behaviors were pointed out and discussed with the supervisee, he acknowledged them, although he was unable to keep himself from engaging in them. The student was not open to exploring the origins of his anxiety in supervision, and he resisted suggestions to pursue therapy (the program had a policy against mandating it). After 2 years of similar behaviors with patients (and, we might add, supervisors), the student dropped out of the program and chose another career path. Our intent here is neither to pontificate nor to chastise but rather to underscore the serious and sometimes severe consequences of countertransference that is not well managed.

On a more optimistic note, there appear to be a number of therapist qualities that minimize the likelihood of countertransference adversely affecting one's work. In previous writings, we have developed, tested, and refined a theory of countertransference management based on five therapist characteristics. The essence of the theory is that problematic countertransference reactions are less likely to occur when therapists possess more self-insight, conceptualizing skills, empathy, self-integration, and anxiety management skills.

The first of these factors, self-insight, may be the most fundamental. Socrates' counsel to "Know thyself" is as relevant today as it was when the phrase was inscribed above the oracle's cave in Delphi. Gurdjieff (1973) underscored the importance of the Greek philosopher's maxim:

> If a man reasons and thinks soundly, no matter what path he follows ... he must inevitably arrive back at himself, and begin with the solution of the problem of what he is himself and what his place is in the world around him. For without this knowledge, he will have no focal point in his search. Socrates' words "Know thyself" remain for all those who seek true knowledge. (p. 43)

One of the reasons why self-insight is particularly essential for therapists is because our understanding of others is limited by the extent to which we understand ourselves. Therapy is an inherently subjective enterprise, and it requires of the therapist a familiarity with his or her internal landscape. Freud himself asserted that no patient develops further than his or her analyst's neuroses (Freud, 1910/1959). He wrote

> It does not suffice ... that the pysician should be of approximate normality himself; it is a justifiable requsition that he should ... become aware of those complexes in himself which would be apt to affect his comprehension of the patient's disclosures. (1912/1959b, p. 159)

Freud was implying that, at a minimum, therapists should seek to understand themselves and, preferably, work to resolve problematic countertransference issues. Along these lines, Robertiello and Schoenewolf (1987) advised "we should be the constant objects of our own observation, looking for any intense feelings about patients, and being vigilant about what the next instant will be in which our unconscious may betray us" (p. 290).

Acquiring self-insight is an extremely difficult process, however. Thoreau wrote that perceiving oneself accurately is as difficult as seeing behind oneself without turning around. It is easier to see behind oneself with assistance, of course, by using an unclouded mirror, for instance, or with the help of someone with a different perspective. But even with the aid of another, humans can evidence remarkable resistance to self-insight (Castonguay & Hill, 2006). One of the primary reasons for this resistance is fear. Maslow (1968) believed that among Freud's greatest contributions was his idea that we are afraid to know ourselves. We fear what we do not know. We prefer the familiarity of our constructions of ourselves—or others' constructions of ourselves that have been internalized—than more that accurate self-perceptions. On some level, we recognize and resist the truth in Ouspensky's (1949) assertion "Self-observation brings man to the realization of the necessity for change" (p. 145). Many forces in addition to fear operate against self-insight: habit, addiction, preoccupation with trivia, societal mesmerism, human predilection for comfort. *Discomfort*, on the other hand, typically is required for self-insight. We need to be shaken up to be awakened, to see ourselves more accurately. Crises can serve this purpose. In fact, life provides no shortage of unpleasant experiences that can serve as opportunities for self-insight. In the words of musician Bruce Springsteen, "Insight is expensive, especially the sudden kind." Gains in awareness are not free; some form of payment is required, and the payment is often uncomfortable.

Aside from taking advantage of situational circumstances or life events, however, are there particular practices that therapists can engage in to further self-awareness? In a qualitative investigation of countertransference management practices, Baehr (2004) interviewed 12 psychologists, several of whom not only identified self-awareness as critical to managing countertransference but also identified activities that facilitated their self-awareness. First, some therapists found it useful to spend time engaging in periods of what might be described as a kind of free-floating reflection. Therapists described almost unintentionally thinking about some aspect of themselves. This might occur while showering, exercising, driving, or preparing for a session. For example, one therapist said that prior to seeing a patient, she was ruminating about her general level of compassion. She reported finding this introspection beneficial in that it helped her avoid getting angry and "sucked in" (p. 164) by the patient. A second practice that was identified as promoting therapist self-awareness was meditation. The practice of meditation, in any number of forms, can enhance mindfulness, or a moment-to-moment awareness of what one is experiencing (Kabat-Zinn, 2003). The more that therapists are able to observe their thoughts, feelings, and behaviors, the better able they will be to derive insight into themselves. A final kind of practice that was identified by therapists in Baehr's (2004) study as helpful to self-awareness was termed *self-care.* Therapists described how they tended to be less self-aware when they felt run-down or burned out and, conversely, how they seemed to be more self-aware when they felt rejuvenated by reading for pleasure, limiting the number of patients seen in a day, going to professional conferences, and resting.

Given the largely unconscious origins of countertransference, the more aware therapists are of their motivations, needs, conflicts, and desires, the less likely they are to act unintentionally. Of course, self-understanding is not a static concept; knowledge of one's self fluctuates over time. But whether considered from a longer term or moment-to-moment perspective, self-insight helps therapists manage their conflicts, vulnerabilities, and soft spots. Research supports this notion, but not as consistently as one might expect. On one hand, psychotherapy experts rate self-insight to be an important component of countertransference management (J. A. Hayes et al., 1991), and therapists consider self-insight to distinguish excellent from average clinicians (Van Wagoner et al., 1991). However, several studies have failed to detect a relationship between therapists' self-insight and both countertransference behavior (Gelso et al., 1995) and therapy outcome (Gelso et al., 2001; J. A. Hayes, Riker, & Ingram, 1997).

Additional research provides clues as to why therapists' self-insight may be insufficient in preventing countertransference behavior. Two different studies found that therapists displayed less countertransference behavior when they had an awareness of their countertransference feelings and were able to use a theoretical structure to understand their reactions to patients (Latts & Gelso, 1995; Robbins & Jolkovski, 1987). In other words, to prevent negative countertransference behavior, it may be necessary for therapists to have enough self-insight to know that they are experiencing countertransference feelings and also to have sufficient conceptualizing abilities to know what to do with these reactions. Reich (1951) described this process as locating an "outside position in order to be capable of an objective evaluation of what [was] just now felt within" (p. 25). Even when considered independently of self-insight, conceptualizing skills are likely to help prevent displays of negative countertransference reactions in that they provide an intellectual framework for understanding these reactions and perhaps how to contain them. This may be particularly true when working with more severely disturbed patients who may stir a host of issues in virtually any therapist. For example, patients with borderline personality features are notorious at arousing negative reactions in therapists, in part because they are so adept at honing in on and provoking vulnerabilities within the therapist. The more the therapist takes such patient behavior personally, the more likely she or he is to react in a nonproductive fashion. On the other hand, when the therapist can conceptualize the patient's behavior more objectively, for example, as an attempt to recreate familiar relationship dynamics, the therapist is less likely to react in a countertherapeutic manner. We would note with caution that when taken to an extreme, a therapist's use of conceptualizing ability to manage countertransference can assume the form of defensive intellectualization. Countertransference is never purely a function of the patient and his or her traits, diagnosis, or behavior. Countertransference always results from some mix of therapist and patient characteristics, and thus therapists' conceptualizations of countertransference and its management must involve themselves. This sort of personal involvement in conceptualizing countertransference dynamics limits the defensive intellectualizing tendency.

In addition to self-insight and conceptualizing skills, another therapist factor thought to facilitate countertransference management is empathy. As a number of theoreticians have described, empathy requires a partial or provisional identification with the patient (Beres & Arlow, 1974; Greenson, 1960; A. Reich, 1951; Slakter, 1987). Over- or underidentification can lead to, or result from, countertransference. For example, in a study in which countertransference was defined in terms of distorted perceptions of patients' personalities, McClure and Hodge (1987) found that therapists who strongly liked their patients tended to misperceive patients as overly similar to themselves, and therapists who strongly disliked their patients tended to misperceive patients as overly dissimilar from themselves. Empathy helps provide a middle-ground perspective. The therapist who is able to stay attuned to the patient's communications, feelings, experiences, and needs is less likely to put her or his own needs ahead of the patient's. The empathic therapist can anticipate the consequences on the patient of the therapist's self-serving behavior and is better able to refrain from it.

At the same time, it is important that the therapist not lose a sense of self in the process of engaging empathically with the patient. The patient's therapeutic needs will be undermined when the therapist is overidentified and does not have enough distance from the patient to conceptualize clearly and to offer the patient a perspective other than the patient's own. Research findings support the notion that therapist empathy helps prevent countertransference behavior. J. A. Hayes et al. (1997) found that therapist trainees' empathic ability, as judged by former supervisors, was inversely related to their countertransference behavior with current patients. In addition, Peabody and Gelso (1982) found that empathic ability was positively related to awareness of countertransference feelings, which in turn, was inversely related to the acting out of countertransference. Finally, therapists in Baehr's (2004) qualitative study described the importance of empathizing with patients and seeing them holistically to prevent countertransference behavior. One therapist said, "I feel really strongly that whenever you start dealing with someone as a *them* or an *other* instead of another human being who possesses any potential that you have, then I think that you start getting into all sorts of trouble" (p. 152).

The empathic process just described, of partially and temporarily identifying without becoming fused with patients, requires yet another characteristic in therapists. We have labeled this feature *self-integration* and have come to view it as a critical component of managing countertransference. Self-integration refers to a therapist's having a relatively stable identity, being able to differentiate from others, and generally possessing sound psychological health. As with a dance partner, the therapist must be close enough to the patient to remain in contact while not being so close as to interfere with movement. Although enmeshment might feel good to some patients, and to some therapists as well, effective therapy requires an appropriate distance in the therapy relationship. Therapists must be able to assess and, when necessary, alter the distance between themselves and a patient, and therapists who are better self-integrated will have an easier time with this difficult task. As research has demonstrated, countertransference that arises from areas of unresolved conflict can interfere with psychotherapy process and outcome (J. A. Hayes et al., 1997; J. A. Hayes & Gelso, 1993; J. A. Hayes et al., 1998; Ligiero & Gelso, 2002; Rosenberger & Hayes, 2002). Therefore, therapists who have fewer conflicts, or whose conflicts are more resolved, are less likely to experience problematic countertransference. Baehr (2004) describes a case that provides an illustration of the manner in which a therapist's unresolved conflicts can interfere with therapy:

> Due to her mother's reaction to having a stillborn child when the therapist was two, as well as other factors, the therapist had a history of not feeling cherished. She also felt overwhelmed by the impact of her divorce several years before. The client had a severe abuse history and resulting dissociative disorder, expressing itself in almost complete silence in therapy. Together these factors led the therapist to wish for respite and feel overwhelmed and frustrated, as well as doubting her ability to help others. The therapist ... had some difficulty joining with the client out of fear of getting lost in a merger of her experiences and the client's. In frustration at her client's silence, the therapist would become almost punitively silent at times. This was a repetition of the perpetrator–victim relationship for the client. The therapist was struggling to stay present but really felt like sleeping. The client remained disengaged as long as she didn't feel the therapist joining her.

The last of the five factors, *anxiety management*, has been implicated in both theory and research as central to countertransference management. "Anxiety," Freud (1926/1959) posited, "is a reaction to a situation of danger. It is obviated by the ego's doing something to avoid that situation or to withdraw from it" (pp. 128–129). Similarly, Sullivan (1954) believed "Not only does no one want anxiety, but if it is present, the lessening of it is always desirable, except under the most extraordinary circumstances. Anxiety is a sign that something ought to be different at once" (p. 100). Cohen (1952) conceived of anxiety as indicative of the presence of countertransference, a view that has received empirical support. A number of studies have found that both trait anxiety and state anxiety are predictors of countertransference behavior, and state anxiety consistently and successfully has been operationalized as an emotional manifestation of countertransference (Gelso et al., 1995; J. A. Hayes et al., 1998; J. A. Hayes & Gelso, 1991, 1993; Yulis & Kiesler, 1968). In other words, anxiety is both an internal state that predicts external countertransference behavior and, in and of itself, it has been found to be an emotional marker of countertransference. It is plausible to assume, then, that therapists who are better able to manage their anxiety are less likely to experience countertransference behavior, and therapists who are less prone to anxiety will experience less of it when their conflicts or vulnerabilities are stimulated. Research generally has upheld this proposition (Fauth & Williams, 2005; Gelso et al., 1995; Gelso et al., 2002; J. A. Hayes & Gelso, 1991; Yulis & Kiesler, 1968), though not without exception (Hayes et al., 1997). Anecdotally, we have found more than a few novice therapists to be so anxious about their clinical performance that they undermine their very attempts to be helpful. An effective, paradoxical supervisory intervention with these trainees is to point out their narcissism, however unintended it may be. Calling attention to the trainee's excessive concern with his or her own performance tends to help supervisees return more of their focus to the patient's welfare.

These five factors—self-insight, conceptualizing ability, empathy, self-integration, and anxiety management—can be thought of not only as therapist qualities that facilitate the management of countertransference but as actual constituents of the countertransference management process. That is, they are part and parcel of what the therapist does to manage countertransference in the therapy hour. Let us examine each of the five factors to see how this is so. With regard to self-insight, for example, the therapist must maintain an awareness of what she is experiencing during a session to manage her countertransference feelings and thoughts and keep them from spilling over into countertransference behavior. When an awareness of his or her internal experience is lacking, the therapist is more likely to act out in countertransferential ways. At the same time, this self-awareness can be coupled with a conceptual understanding of one's reactions to minimize their adverse influences on the work. Still further, by remaining empathically attuned to the patient, the therapist may be able to anticipate the effects on the patient of acting on his or her countertransference impulses and thereby refrain from doing so. The very act of empathizing, in other words, may reduce countertransference behavior. However, the therapist needs to be careful not to go beyond empathy and become overidentified. Self-integration is important here. Maintaining appropriate boundaries and retaining a sense of self, separate from the patient, in the therapeutic hour will help therapists own their reactions and take responsibility for their moment-to-moment behavior. Finally, managing one's anxiety while conducting therapy is central to managing countertransference so that the therapist does not become emotionally removed from the patient or allow the anxiety to otherwise interfere with optimal therapeutic performance.

REMEDIATING THE NEGATIVE EFFECTS OF COUNTERTRANSFERENCE

Whereas the preceding paragraphs address countertransference management from a preventive perspective, next we take a remedial approach in discussing how to deal with the damage that has occurred due to problematic countertransference behavior.

The same cluster of five therapist characteristics—self-insight, conceptualizing skills, empathy, self-integration, and anxiety management—are relevant here as well. In this section, we consider these factors, particularly in conjunction with one another, in minimizing the harm that can result from negative countertransference behavior.

To begin, self-insight is likely to facilitate the therapist's understanding of why countertransference has occurred. By knowing the specific conflicts or vulnerabilities in oneself that were provoked, therapists are in a position to disclose the basis for their countertransference, if they think such a disclosure will be beneficial to the patient. Although such decisions are largely a matter of clinical judgment, research in this area may be useful to consider. One study suggests that if the working alliance is strong, patients tend to perceive personal therapist disclosures favorably, although for patients who are relatively unfamiliar with the therapy process, specific countertransference disclosures may be contraindicated. Also, if the working alliance is weak, countertransference disclosures do not seem to be constructive (Myers & Hayes, 2006).

Because countertransference is a function of both therapist and patient factors, therapist self-insight is not likely to be sufficient in understanding its causes. Therapists' conceptualizing skills will be valuable in discerning the specific patient, relational, and contextual factors that contribute to the countertransference reaction. In addition, conceptualizing skills may be useful in identifying and making sense of the intrapsychic origins of one's countertransference. For example, we know of a cognitive-behaviorally oriented colleague who admittedly has difficulty setting limits with patients. This can take the form of spontaneously extended sessions, late-night phone calls from patients, and readily reduced fees. The therapist recognizes this as a chronic countertransference issue and tends to conceive of it in terms of a core schema related to being perfect (e.g., placing others' needs first) and, by extension, being a perfect therapist (e.g., always being available). If he were a person-centered therapist, he might usefully conceptualize these same countertransference issues in terms of internalized conditions of worth (i.e., "I am a good person if I place others' needs ahead of my own"). The particular framework itself is less important than its utility to the therapist as a means of understanding the origins of one's countertransference reactions, their effects, and how to manage them.

Whether or not the therapist is able to pinpoint the causes of a particular countertransference reaction, her or his empathy is likely to be an asset in determining how to repair the damage that might have occurred to the patient, therapy relationship, or treatment. The patient may communicate, subtly or otherwise, the effects on him or her of the therapist's countertransference, and the challenge to the therapist is to recover from the self-serving countertransference behavior and shift the focus back to empathizing with the patient. Therapists who have greater self-integration can extricate themselves more quickly from such a countertransferential web and direct their attention back to the patient. For example, one of the authors had been working for a number of years with a patient who had a history of severe sexual abuse. Thinking he could not possibly hear anything more traumatic than what the patient had already shared, the therapist was caught off guard one day when the patient began to describe a horrific account of abuse. The therapist's reaction was to pull back emotionally and launch into an atypical, highly intellectualized monologue along the lines of "Yes, well, we'll have to look at those issues closely and determine the feelings you have that are associated with them and then apply the coping strategies that we've been discussing in here and ..." The patient cut him off. "What are you doing?" she asked. (Fortunately, they had developed a strong enough relationship that she could be so blunt.) Upon momentary reflection, it occurred to the therapist that he was protecting himself—from the awfulness of what he was about to hear, from the patient's feelings, and from his own anxiety. The therapist chose to disclose some of his internal experience and used his anxiety to relate empathically to how difficult it was for the patient to recall and prepare to discuss the traumatic incident. The therapist then was able to stay fairly connected to the patient as she explored this painful memory.

The realization that one has acted out in potentially harmful ways can generate a fair amount of anxiety, even among seasoned clinicians, so managing one's anxiety is an important element in making repairs following countertransference behavior. This is especially true if a therapist decides to discuss what has occurred with the patient. The judicious route may be to not pursue such a discussion, depending on the patient's ability to process interpersonal material, the strength of the alliance, the phase of therapy, and other factors. Then again, therapists need to be as clear as possible that not discussing countertransference with a patient is not more a matter of ease or self-protection than clinical judgment. We would agree with the position taken by Jung (1963) when he wrote, "When important matters are at stake, it makes all the difference whether the doctor sees himself as a part of the drama, or cloaks himself in his authority" (p. 133).

In addition to particular therapist traits that may be helpful in remediating the negative effects of countertransference, are there other factors that may be of assistance to therapists? In the aforementioned qualitative study of 12 therapists, Baehr (2004) found that relationships, both personal and professional, were important to a number of therapists. These relationships served a number of functions. First, they were "containers" for therapists' emotional reactions to patients. For example, one therapist noted that regular consultation with colleagues allowed him to accept his anger toward a patient rather than disowning it, in part because he noticed his colleagues' angry reactions on his behalf as he described his patients' behavior. Second, the therapist's personal and professional relationships can facilitate a deeper understanding of the therapist's reactions to patients. Trusted others can serve as a sounding board and a source of feedback for therapists as they sort through difficult and occasionally confusing reactions to clients. For example, therapists in Baehr's (2004) study reported that colleagues and loved ones helped therapists (a) make connections between their reactions and their own personal histories, (b) their needs, (c) their interpersonal tendencies, (d) ways in which patients were similar to therapists, (e) ways in which patients were similar to significant others in therapists' lives, and (f) a variety of patient factors. Finally, Baehr found that close relationships can provide unconditional support to the therapist that the therapist can, and often does, internalize and subsequently offer to the patient. For example, one therapist believed that her marriage allowed her to relate more deeply and genuinely with her patients. In her words, "just being in a relationship where I feel secure and I feel like ... he knows the worst of me and we've gotten to the point in our relationship where we can confront each other ... I feel safe in that sense" (p. 163).

MAKING THERAPEUTIC USE OF THE POSITIVE ASPECTS OF COUNTERTRANSFERENCE

Up to this point in the chapter, we have been addressing how to deal with countertransference when it assumes the form of a master. How can a therapist prevent becoming controlled by countertransference and how can one minimize the harmful consequences once control has been lost? For the remainder of the chapter, we turn our attention to the ways in which therapists might intentionally use countertransference in the service of their work with patients.

The idea that individuals' conflicts or vulnerabilities might be therapeutic to others is an ancient concept referred to in many literatures as the "wounded healer." According to Jackson (2001), the notion of the wounded healer refers to:

> The inner "woundedness" of a healer—the healer's own suffering and vulnerability, which have been said to contribute crucially to the capacity to heal. I am thus referring to healers whose personal experiences of illness have left lingering effects on them—in the form of lessons learned that later serve constructive purposes, in the form of attitudes and sensitivities that recurrently serve them in ministering to those whom they treat, or in the form of symptoms or characteristics that stay with them and usefully influence their therapeutic endeavors. That is to say, these healers' own experiences as sufferers may have an enhancing or useful effect on their healing capacities. (p. 2)

Healing practices based on the notion of the wounded healer can be found in a variety of societies and approaches to treatment. For example, shamanistic cultures around the world have been known to appoint as healers individuals who have suffered some type of physical or emotional wound. The underlying belief is that "the wound validates the healer's ability to move 'between the worlds'—the world of the well and the world of the ill, for it is in the bridging of these worlds that the healing power lies" (Halifax, 1982, p. 84). This same idea can be found in approaches to drug and alcohol treatment that are based on the principle that treatment is more effective when offered by individuals who themselves have recovered from addiction (White, 2000). The concept of the wounded healer also can be found in the field of pastoral counseling, as expressed, for example, by Nouwen (1972): "A deep understanding of one's own pain makes it possible to convert weakness into strength and to offer one's own experience as a source of healing to those who are often lost in the darkness of their own misunderstood sufferings" (p. 87).

The concept of the wounded healer has been advocated by prominent psychotherapists as well. For instance, in an interview shortly before his death, Rogers (2000) said,

> I am inclined to think that in my writing perhaps I have stressed too much the three basic conditions. ... The therapist needs to recognize very clearly the fact that he or she is an imperfect person with flaws which make him vulnerable. I think it is only as the therapist views himself as imperfect and flawed that he can see himself as helping another person. (p. 34)

This is a rather remarkable statement considering that Rogers's writing on the three basic conditions spanned five decades. Here, reflecting upon his life's work, Rogers suggests that he underemphasized the importance of therapists perceiving themselves as imperfect and flawed, as having conflicts and vulnerabilities, as being human. Jung (1963) expressed this same sentiment in his well-known statement, "Only the wounded physician heals" (p. 134). Jung went on to write,

> The patient's treatment begins with the doctor, so to speak. Only if the doctor knows how to cope with himself and his own problems will he be able to teach the patient to do the same. ... I will be forced to pay attention to my own sufferings and needs if I am to be of service to anyone else. (p. 132)

Jung clearly was speaking from personal experience. In his autobiography, he wrote openly about his difficulties with his father's authoritarianism, his mother's instability, and his own feelings of loneliness, inadequacy, and having split personas.

Historically, the concept of the wounded healer can be traced back to Greek mythology and the character of Chiron, the centaur. Chiron's father, Saturn, had romantic interests in a woman named Philyra, who resisted his attempts to pursue her. At one point, she turned herself into a horse to evade Saturn. Aware of Philyra's actions, Saturn disguised himself as a horse, a sexual encounter ensued, and Chiron, born half human and half horse, was the result. Saturn disavowed his child-rearing responsibilities, and Philyra, upon seeing Chiron's grotesque appearance, pleaded with the gods to be turned into a linden tree rather than to raise her son. Wounded at birth by his father's abandonment and his mother's rejection, Chiron was raised by Apollo, the god of music, prophecy, and healing. Chiron himself became skilled in the healing arts as he matured. Eventually, he mentored Asclepius, considered to be the founder of Greek medicine, as well as other notable figures in Greek mythology, including Jason, Achilles, and Hercules.

According to legend, Hercules accidentally shot Chiron with a poisoned arrow and produced an agonizing wound that neither Chiron nor anyone else was able to cure. Owing to his father's status as a god, Chiron was immortal and therefore faced eternal suffering. Chiron then retreated to the cave in which he dwelled, engaged in a period of deep introspection, and emerged with a renewed desire to heal others. Eventually, Chiron's own suffering was too much for him to bear, and he gave his immortality to a human being, Prometheus, so that he [Chiron] might die and Prometheus have life eternal. The gods cast Chiron into the heavens in the form of the constellation Sagitarrius (Jackson, 2001; Reinhart, 1989; Snodgrass, 1994; Whan, 1987).

In overcoming his wounds and then engaging teaching and healing practices, Chiron illustrates the notion that it is possible for individuals to use their experiences of suffering for the benefit of others. Perhaps the most promising and compelling element of this premise is the basic fact that all human beings suffer; consequently, we all are potential healers. Of course, suffering itself does not necessarily promote healing. As Nouwen (1972) wrote, "Open wounds stink and do not heal" (p. 88). The essential factor is to resolve one's suffering sufficiently so that it might be beneficial to others. This alchemical process—transforming the lead of the therapist's life into gold for patients—is at the heart of utilizing countertransference in therapy.

For example, a patient of one of the authors had been trying for quite a number of years to conceive a child. When she discovered that she finally was pregnant, her elation was palpable. So, too, was her sorrow when, several weeks later, the patient learned that she had miscarried; she was emotionally devastated. Upon hearing the news, the therapist was taken back to his own experience, years earlier, when he and his wife had experienced a miscarriage at a similarly advanced stage of pregnancy. The grief was devastating, nearly overwhelming. The author and his wife had named the baby, felt her kicks, dreamed of what she would look like, readied their home and their lives for her arrival. The author's sorrow took root in fields plowed by earlier experiences of loss in his life. It was primarily from this personal vantage point that the patient's suffering was understood. It was also the case that the therapist could offer a deep and genuine sense of hope to the patient that her pain would subside eventually, and he explored with her ways to ritualize her grief, including some options that had been helpful to him. In the words of the 14th century Italian poet Petrarca, "No one's solace penetrates a saddened mind more than that of a fellow sufferer, and therefore the most effective words to strengthen the spirits of bystanders are those which emerge from the actual torments" (Jackson, 2001, p. 8).

It should be noted that, in the aforementioned example, it was especially critical for the therapist to recognize the unique features of the patient and her miscarriage and not overgeneralize from his own personal experience. Doing so can result in empathic failure, as when the therapist mistakenly assumes that he or she knows exactly what the patient is talking about, feeling, or thinking because the therapist has "been there" previously. In sum, then, while it can be helpful for a therapist to have some life experience in common with a patient, it is crucial that the therapist not blur the distinctions between the patient's experience and his or her own.

That being said, it seems important for therapists to see both themselves and patients within a wounded healer framework. Therapists who deny their own conflicts and vulnerabilities are at risk of projecting onto patients the persona of "the wounded one" and seeing themselves as "the one who is healed." When this dichotomy is established, therapists cannot use their own experiences of suffering to empathize with patients, and patients' inner healing capacities are not acknowledged and utilized (Guggenbuhl-Craig, 1971; Laskowski & Pellicore, 2002). "There is no essential difference between the two people engaged in a healing relationship. Indeed, both are wounded and both are healers. It is the woundedness of the healer which enables him or her to understand the patient and which informs the wise and healing action" (Remen, May, Young, & Berland, 1985, p. 85). Consistent with this view, Yalom (2002) notes, "We are all in this together and there is no therapist and no person immune to the inherent tragedies of existence" (p. 8).

Empirical research on the notion of the wounded healer is limited, and what little data exist are mixed. Studies tend not to support the popular belief that drug and alcohol treatment is more effective when offered by therapists in recovery (Culbreth, 2000; Najavits & Weiss, 1994). Much of this research, however, is confounded by the fact that therapists in recovery tend to be less well-educated and trained than therapists who are not in recovery. Unless therapists' educational status is accounted for, it is difficult to determine the potential effects of therapists' recovery status. In addition, sobriety does not guarantee resolution of one's internal conflicts that underlie addictive behavior. Nonetheless, according to one qualitative study, it is not unusual for therapists to attribute their effectiveness to the resolution of personal suffering (Wolgien & Coady, 1997). This brings us back to the five-factor model of countertransference management that was discussed earlier in the chapter. What is their relationship to the concept of wounded healer? Might these same five therapist characteristics help therapists to use their countertransference intentionally and beneficially? We conclude the chapter by exploring these questions.

Let us begin with therapist's self-insight. As the term implies, insight requires the ability to see, which in turn, requires light. Colloquial expressions reveal the metaphorical connection between understanding and sight, as in "to be enlightened," "to see the light," or "to shed light on a problem." On the other hand, when one is "in the dark" about something, one lacks understanding. Interestingly, this was not always the case. Bly (1988) notes that prior to the 13th century, when the word insight originated, there was recognition that "darkness contains intelligence and nourishment and even information" (p. 42). In any event, to use themselves, including their countertransference, as therapeutic instruments, therapists must be able to see into themselves, to understand their fluctuating needs and preferences and shortcomings and longings. Self-insight is a necessary precondition for connecting one's own experiences with a patient's experience. Intentionally drawing from one's personal history in one's work with patients is demanding and, ultimately, rewarding. According to Maeder (1989), a therapist's decision to become immersed in clinical work on more than an intellectual level

> leads to a painful confrontation with his own problems and weaknesses, and ultimately to self-knowledge. Ideally, he can overcome the difficulties; at worst, he may be forced to resign himself to insuperable handicaps. In either case, though, the end result is a clearer perception of his ambitions and needs and their relationship to the task at hand. He can approach others with honesty, compassion, and humility, knowing that he is motivated by genuine concern, not by some ulterior motive. (p. 77)

Supposing that a therapist has the requisite self-knowledge to use countertransference effectively to benefit her or his work, a pertinent question then is how to actually do so. Conceptualizing skills and empathy seem to be key ingredients in the process (Barrett-Lennard, 1981; Greenberg & Rushanki-Rosenberg, 2000; Hatcher et al., 2005; Kohut, 1959; Mahrer, Boulet, & Fairweather, 1994; Rogers, 1975). Using the work of these authors as a base, we present a three-step model for using countertransference in one's work.

The first step involves the therapist creating an environment that is conducive to the patient's open sharing and the therapist's empathic relating. The second step requires more elaboration than the first. As the patient is communicating, the therapist finds internal "reference points," or memories and images from his or her personal history, that "provide a bridge via which empathic attunement may be achieved" (Hatcher et al., 2005, p. 200). In other words, the therapist's personal experience—including conflicts that have been adequately resolved—serves as a source of connection and understanding.

It should be noted that the content of the reference point does not need to match the patient's material. Taken to its logical extreme, this would require therapists to experience every problem faced by their patients. Although it may be useful for the therapist to have shared experiences in common with the patient, it may suffice for the therapist to locate a reference point that is characterized by affect that is similar to the patient's. For instance, whereas a therapist who has worked through the death of a parent may be particularly able to understand a patient whose parent has died, any one of a number of loss issues in the therapist's life may effectively serve as a reference point for empathizing with the patient. Furthermore, if the patient is feeling rage at the deceased parent and anger was not an emotion the therapist felt after his or her parent died, the therapist is probably better off searching for a personal experience of rage from which to connect to and understand the patient.

Hatcher et al. (2005) provide helpful examples in which therapists used experiences from their own past to understand patients. For instance, in relating to an agoraphobic, nausea-prone patient who had a critical father, one therapist described how she drew from similar life experiences to empathize with the patient. "In junior high school I was so afraid of being made fun of by the other kids, I would get nauseous at recess. I found any and all excuses not to go to recess" (p. 204). Another therapist commented, "When he was explaining his concern that his race may actually be a factor in his lack of positive job appraisal, I related to my own experience of suspecting I did not get a position I was well qualified for due to my gender" (p. 206). And a third therapist noted, "Oh my gosh, this is my mother-in-law...I may have been identifying with her and also with one of her children" (p. 206).

It is worth repeating here that empathic failure can result from overidentifying with patients' experiences, and so caution is called for in walking the "use-of-self tightrope." For example, a female colleague of ours who was about to get married was working with a woman seeking therapy for difficulties with her new husband. The therapist, seemingly unaware of her identification with the patient, consistently deflected and minimized the patient's concerns, advised the patient to stay with the marriage, and reassured her repeatedly that "everything would work out." Personal involvement in the work, whether intentional, or as was the case here, unintentional, can evoke anxiety. Therapists who can manage their anxiety can stay with the process of using countertransference intentionally in their work.

In the third step of the process, the therapist takes into account factors such as timing, content, tone, affect, and the patient's capacity to receive what the therapist wishes to convey, and then engages in empathic expression. This communication may or may not involve the therapist's disclosure of the internal reference point that was used to understand the patient. Again, this is a matter of clinical judgment, and prescriptions and generalities seem unwise.

It almost goes without saying that to engage in this process of using oneself so intensively in the work requires the therapist to be psychologically healthy. In terms of the five-factor model that we have been using throughout the chapter, this is a matter of self-integration. The therapist's wounds need to be sufficiently healed to be drawn from usefully. We would argue that one's vulnerabilities and conflicts are never fully resolved, nor do they need to be. In fact, a therapist's issues probably need to be alive enough so that they are available to be drawn upon in the work. Conflicts that are dormant or sealed off cannot be used to relate to the patient. The ideal, then, would be for therapists to be more healed than wounded, to be able to empathize with patients' woundedness and to offer patients a lived sense of potential healing.

CONCLUSION

It has been said that countertransference is the best of servants, but the worst of masters. The challenges in managing countertransference so that it serves rather than dominates one's work are complex and formidable. Several therapist characteristics seem to facilitate this process: self-insight, conceptualizing ability, empathy, self-integration, and anxiety management. Therapists can seek to function as wounded healers in the ideal sense by drawing from their own experiences of working through painful personal incidents to better understand, offer hope to, and work therapeutically with patients.

6

Empirical Research on Countertransference

In 1958, the preeminent and pioneering psychotherapy researcher Hans Strupp wrote, "The therapist himself, his background, attitudes, experiences, and personality must be put under the microscope for careful scrutiny and analysis if valid knowledge about how to treat mental illness is to be obtained" (p. 34). With this rather bold statement, Strupp asserted that therapist factors, personal therapist factors, needed to be understood as part of a knowledge base about effective psychotherapy. Despite Strupp's foresight, it has taken the field of psychotherapy research nearly half a century to recognize the wisdom of his statement. Prior to the turn of the 21st century, the success of psychotherapy outcome typically was attributed to three factors in the research literature: patient variables, techniques, and common factors (i.e., those that are germane across all theoretical approaches, such as the working alliance and Rogers's necessary and sufficient conditions). Research on the personal (i.e., nontherapy specific) qualities of the therapist, when it was present at all, was devoted primarily to superficial variables such as the sex or age of the therapist. Not surprisingly, these variables, whose influence on the process of psychotherapy is fairly removed, did not account for much variability in psychotherapy outcome, thereby furthering the belief that factors related to the person of the therapist are relatively unimportant in determining therapeutic success. To our way of thinking, the therapist's vulnerabilities and unresolved conflicts constitute personal qualities that exact greater influence on the process of therapy than more distal variables such as the therapist's sex and age.

The empirically supported and manualized treatment movement in the late 20th century initially worsened the state of affairs as far as therapist factors are concerned. The empirically supported treatment movement attempted to validate, for a variety of patient problems and disorders, particular approaches to therapy characterized by specific techniques. The emphasis on technical factors as responsible for patient change contributed to the field's neglect of therapist variables. However, in response to the widespread popularity of empirically supported treatments, important counterarguments were generated about nontechnical factors responsible for therapeutic change (Westen, Novotny, & Thompson-Brenner, 2004). Wampold's (2001) critical analysis of the psychotherapy research literature, for example, demonstrated rather convincingly that therapist factors accounted for more variability in outcome than did the actual techniques upon which manualized treatments are based. In fact, when therapist factors are accounted for, the effects of techniques on outcome nearly disappear. Of course, Wampold's conclusions are consistent with what every clinician knows: Some therapists are simply better than others. Investigations into personal therapist variables that might account for differential effectiveness have been limited, however.

Knowledge of how therapists' backgrounds, personalities, and experiences affect their work with patients has been based almost exclusively on therapists' personal reflections and anecdotes. Therapists often share their experiences and knowledge with trusted colleagues with whom they work closely, but much of this valuable clinical wisdom accrues, and atrophies, in the offices of individual therapists. It has been difficult to generate and retain a collective, cumulative wisdom about the person of the therapist because this information is transmitted so infrequently in public forums (e.g., symposia, workshops, and professional books and articles).

Therapists' reluctance to publicly share their vulnerabilities and conflicts is understandably human. Doing so is an act of beneficence that requires tremendous courage. Therapists' reticence to disclose their personal soft spots is compounded by the taboo nature of countertransference that still prevails, owing originally to Freud's view of countertransference as neurotically based and detrimental to therapy. Nonetheless, even if a cumulative knowledge base were to be established from therapists sharing more information about themselves, that which can be gleaned from anecdotal reports runs the risk of yielding idiosyncratic truths that don't generalize widely to other therapists and cases. The goal of research, including research on countertransference, is to discover nominal laws that might apply to more than single cases. Of course, the clinical utility and ultimate value of any empirically discovered truths always is determined at the individual case level. However, by aggregating across cases, countertransference research aims to test hypotheses and discover knowledge about factors that shape the direction and outcome of therapy, sometimes in powerful and subtle ways.

Other than a few sporadic, though important, attempts to study countertransference in the 1950s and 1960s, understanding of countertransference was not informed by research until the 1980s. Research evidence has now accumulated to the point where we can begin to draw from the empirical literature in ways that might inform practice. In this chapter, we review the empirical literature on countertransference, organizing findings according to clinically oriented questions and themes. The chapter concludes with a discussion of what we believe to be the important questions that have yet to be addressed empirically. Throughout the chapter, we summarize, critique, synthesize, and extrapolate from the empirical literature while writing for our fellow therapists. We also hope to provide enough detail to satisfy our fellow researchers, while stimulating the curiosities of those who want to know more and will take it upon themselves to delve into particular studies that we describe.

WHAT DO WE KNOW ABOUT COUNTERTRANSFERENCE FROM EMPIRICAL RESEARCH?

In this section, we summarize in clinically oriented fashion findings from studies on countertransference. We particularly emphasize those findings for which there is empirical support from more than one study. At the same time, we take into account the strengths and limitations of each study in weighing their results and implications for the practice of psychotherapy.

Countertransference Can and Does Emanate From the Therapist's Unresolved Psychological Conflicts

On one hand, the empirical finding that countertransference stems from unresolved conflicts seems rather obvious. After all, the very essence of countertransference, as discussed in previous chapters, involves therapists' conflicts; and a working definition of countertransference that implicates therapist conflicts has been used in most, though not all, research on countertransference. At the same time, the very study of therapists' conflictual issues is enough to give one pause. The challenges in recruiting therapists to participate in research on countertransference are outnumbered only by the difficulties in accurately measuring therapists' conflicts. Therapists need to be both willing and able to accurately report their conflicts, or creative efforts that don't rely on self-report need to be used to assess therapists' issues (J. A. Hayes, 2004). Some studies have focused on therapist characteristics that are relatively easy for therapists to report, such as their homophobia (Gelso et al., 1995; J. A. Hayes & Gelso, 1993). The word "relatively" should be emphasized here because some therapists are not fully aware of their homophobia and, in an environment of political correctness, some therapists may be inclined to respond to such measures in a socially desirable way. Other studies have attempted to identify countertransference origins by assessing therapists' blind spots (Cutler, 1958; Rosenberger & Hayes, 2002). Still other studies have relied on straightforward interviews with therapists that inquire about the bases for their countertransference (e.g., J. A. Hayes et al., 1998). Taken as a whole, research has demonstrated that countertransference can emanate from issues related to a therapist's family of origin, narcissism, roles as a parent and romantic partner, unmet needs, grandiosity, and professional self-concept. Related to this last point, for example, one therapist who had a need to "look good" professionally distanced himself emotionally from a patient whose treatment was not progressing (J. A. Hayes et al., 1998). It is safe to say that countertransference can originate from virtually any area of unresolved conflict within the therapist. These conflicts typically have a developmental nature to them in that they derive from issues in the therapist's past, although not always in readily apparent ways. For instance, a therapist's struggles with termination may be rooted in long-standing fears of intimacy and unresolved wounds related to previous loss experiences (Boyer & Hoffman, 1993; Cruz & Hayes, 2006). The point to be underscored is that the origins of a therapist's countertransference are likely to be multilayered, may be deeply embedded in the therapist's psyche, and may reside outside of awareness.

Patient Factors and Therapy-Related Events Interact With Therapists' Unresolved Issues to Trigger Countertransference

Research has shown that countertransference can be provoked by a host of different patient and therapy-related factors, although these must be considered in conjunction with therapists' countertransference origins.

This is the essential notion of the countertransference interaction hypothesis discussed in chapter 2, namely that countertransference is virtually always caused by some interplay between therapist and patient factors. For example, when patients talk about material that touches upon therapists' unresolved conflicts, therapists often experience internal countertransference reactions and exhibit countertransference behavior (Cutler, 1958; Fauth & Hayes, 2006; Gelso et al., 1995; J. A. Hayes & Gelso, 1991, 1993; J. A. Hayes et al., 1998; Rosenberger & Hayes, 2002; Sharkin & Gelso, 1993). Clinically useful generalizations about the kinds of patient material that will trigger countertransference reactions are difficult to make with any accuracy. Topics that are threatening to one therapist may not be to another, depending upon each therapist's unresolved conflicts. Not only can patient material stimulate countertransference, but so too can changes in the structure of therapy, such as missed appointments, the patient showing up late for sessions, and therapy drawing to a close. In fact, termination can be a common trigger for therapists' countertransference reactions, especially for those with unresolved losses (Boyer & Hoffman, 1993; Cruz & Hayes, 2006; J. A. Hayes et al., 1998). Finally, research has demonstrated that countertransference reactions can be evoked when the patient reminds the therapist of a significant person in the therapist's life, including the therapist himself (or herself). Those similarities may be along the lines of the patient's physical characteristics, although usually deeper personality issues are involved (Baehr, 2004; Fiedler, 1951; J. A. Hayes et al., 1998; McClure & Hodge, 1987; Mohr, Gelso, & Hill, 2005). For example, Mohr et al. (2005) found that countertransference was predicted by the interaction of therapist and patient attachment styles, such that therapists with fearful attachment styles exhibited more distancing countertransference behaviors with patients who had preoccupied as opposed to dismissing attachment styles.

This same interaction between therapist and patient factors is relevant to comprehending the role that cultural factors play with regard to countertransference. A full understanding of the culturally related causes of countertransference can only be gained by taking into account therapist and patient variables (Gelso & Mohr, 2001). For example, knowing that a patient is gay or lesbian tells us relatively little about the likelihood or nature of the therapist's countertransference reactions. In fact, research has found that, in general, therapists are no more likely to experience countertransference reactions in their work with gay and lesbian clients than with heterosexual clients (Gelso et al., 1995; J. A. Hayes & Gelso, 1993). However, these same studies have found that therapist homophobia is strongly predictive of therapists' countertransference reactions to gay and lesbian clients. On the flip side, of course, therapists' homophobia it is not related to countertransference reactions with heterosexual clients. It is only the interaction between the patients' sexual orientation and the therapists' homophobia that is predictive of and allows us to understand something about the therapists' emotional and behavioral reactions. Similarly, therapists' gender and gender-role conflict may play a role in countertransference reactions to male and female patients (Fauth & Hayes, 2006; J. A. Hayes & Gelso, 1991; Peabody & Gelso, 1982; Rosenberger & Hayes, 2002; Yulis & Kiesler, 1968). Research findings suggest that male therapists have a tendency to pull back when their unresolved conflicts are stimulated. Female therapists, in contrast, may be prone to draw nearer to patients, risking enmeshment and overinvolvement, when their unresolved issues are touched upon. Other dimensions of culture such as religion, socioeconomic status, and disability and more importantly, the psychological variables associated with each, have yet to be empirically examined with regard to countertransference.

Countertransference Reactions Exist, and Probably Originate, Internally, in the Form of Private Feelings and Thoughts

As discussed in previous chapters, it is important to distinguish overt displays of countertransference behavior from the more covert, and we suspect, more common types of countertransference reactions that occur within the therapist. The therapist's countertransference-based thoughts and feelings may remain hidden from the patient, and they may provide valuable insight into how the therapist is being affected by the patient. When these internal reactions are not managed and spill over into overt countertransference behavior, the results are less likely to be therapeutic (see text to come).

In terms of affective manifestations of countertransference, one of the most consistent findings in the empirical literature is that anxiety is a common reaction when a therapist's unresolved issues are stimulated (Cruz & Hayes, 2006; Fauth & Hayes, 2006; Gelso et al., 1995; J. A. Hayes et al., 1998; J. A. Hayes & Gelso, 1991, 1993; Latts & Gelso, 1995). These empirical findings are consistent with long-standing clinical theory that suggests that therapist anxiety is a useful and reliable indicator of countertransference (Cohen, 1952). Of course, affective countertransference-based reactions are not limited to anxiety. Hayes et al. (1998) found that therapists' emotional countertransference reactions can take the form of anger, sadness, nurturing feelings, pity, disappointment, inadequacy, boredom, envy, and guilt. For example, one therapist in this study who had unresolved issues around being childless said in a postsession interview, "It may be a matter of countertransference that I got a little bit bored about [the patient's] long-winded tale about the daughter" (p. 476). Furthermore, two studies suggest that therapists are more likely to experience countertransference-based feelings when they are less comfortable with anger in general and when patients direct anger toward the therapist in particular (Bandura et al., 1960; Sharkin & Gelso, 1993).

In terms of cognitive manifestations of countertransference, Cutler's (1958) classic study, discussed previously in chapter 5, indicated that therapists may not accurately remember the frequency with which patients discuss material that is conflictual for the therapist. This finding was not replicated in a study by J. A. Hayes and Gelso (1993) although a subsequent piece of research supported Cutler's study. Specifically, Gelso et al. (1995) detected an interaction between therapist gender and patient sexual orientation in that female therapist trainees had poorer recall of sexual words than did male trainees with a lesbian patient, whereas there were no counselor gender differences for a heterosexual patient. The authors theorized that this was because the female therapists felt more threatened by the patients who were lesbians than did the male therapists. This theorizing is consistent with Freud's (1912/1959b) belief that "Mistakes in recollection occur only at times and in palces where personal consideration has intervened" (p. 155). Related to the notion that therapists' perceptions may be distorted by countertransference, a pair of studies found that therapists might be particularly prone to misperceiving patients as overly similar to or overly dissimilar from themselves when countertransference is operative (Fiedler, 1951; McClure & Hodge, 1987). Finally with regard to cognitive manifestations of countertransference, research suggests that therapists' decisions about treatment itself may be affected when their unresolved issues are provoked (J. A. Hayes et al., 1998). For example, therapists may be more or less active, directive, reactive, and reflective with patients, or may decide to end treatment early as a result of countertransference (J. A. Hayes et al., 1998; Lecours, Bouchard, & Normandin, 1995; Normandin & Bouchard, 1993).

On a Behavioral Level, When Countertransference Is Stimulated, Therapists Often Fail to Maintain an Appropriate Therapeutic Distance With Patients

As discussed in chapter 5, therapy may be likened to a dance. Both require not only engagement with another but also an appropriate distance between those involved. Too little distance and the quality of the movement may be sacrificed as partners become enmeshed. Too much distance and the partners may lose connection with one another. Countertransference reactions often influence the therapist in one of these two directions. A number of studies indicate that when patients talk about material related to therapists' unresolved conflicts, therapists pull back from patients. In fact, therapists' avoidance behavior is the most frequent manifestation of overt countertransference reactions in the empirical literature on countertransference (Bandura et al., 1960; Cutler, 1958; Gelso et al., 1995; J. A. Hayes & Gelso, 1991, 1993; J. A. Hayes et al., 1998; Latts & Gelso, 1995; Lecours et al., 1995; Mohr et al., 2005; Peabody & Gelso, 1982; Robbins & Jolkovski, 1987; Yulis & Kiesler, 1968). Therapists' avoidance can take the form of changing topics, making less personally involving statements (e.g., "You seem angry" vs. "You seem angry with me"), ignoring what a patient has said, and disapproval. For example, J. A. Hayes et al. (1998) found that one therapist's unresolved issues around an impending termination contributed to her avoiding an exploration of the patient's painful affect in the final session of therapy. Although less research has been done on therapists' acting out by drawing too near to patients, several studies do suggest that, at least for some therapists, when patients talk about material related to their unresolved conflicts, therapists do not maintain enough psychological distance with patients (J. A. Hayes et al., 1998; Rosenberger & Hayes, 2002; Williams, Judge, Hill, & Hoffman, 1997). As mentioned already, the therapist's gender may play a role in one's tendency toward under- or overinvolvement with patients when countertransference is stimulated. In particular, most of the research indicating that therapists tend to distance themselves from patients has utilized therapist samples that were exclusively or predominantly men. On the other hand, research suggesting that therapists may respond to conflictual patient material by drawing overly close to patients has been based mainly on studies of women. Again, however, research on overinvolvement is in its infancy, and these gender effects should be viewed as informed speculation in need of further empirical refinement rather than as clinical facts.

Countertransference Behavior Can, but Does not Necessarily, Interfere With Therapy Outcome

Despite a vast amount of theoretical and clinically based literature suggesting that countertransference behavior has an adverse effect on psychotherapy outcome, remarkably few studies have examined this relationship directly. Perhaps even more surprising is the fact that the scant amount of research that has been conducted on the relationship between countertransference and outcome does not support the theoretical and clinical literature in straightforward ways. The only study to date that has directly investigated the possible effects of countertransference behavior on outcome discovered a complex relationship between the two (J. A. Hayes et al., 1997). In this study of 20 cases of brief therapy, countertransference behavior was unrelated to patient improvement as reported by patients, therapists, and therapists' supervisors. However, in cases that had moderate to poor outcome, countertransference behavior was strongly predictive of outcome such that more frequent displays of countertransference behavior were associated with worse outcome. It may be that, in therapy relationships typified by a strong working alliance, which is typically present in cases with good outcome, the relationship can tolerate displays of countertransference behavior. However, when the alliance between the patient and therapist is weak, as is often true when treatment outcome is poor, it may be that countertransference directly contributes to adverse outcome.

Although the direct link between countertransference and outcome has been tested only rarely, the weight of the indirect empirical evidence strongly suggests that countertransference behavior tends to impede outcomes. For example, research has found that countertransference enactments are related to poorer working alliances (Ligiero & Gelso, 2002), which themselves consistently predict worse outcome. In addition, a study by Gelso et al. (2002) provided indirect evidence of the relationship between countertransference and psychotherapy outcome. In this study, therapist trainees who were judged by their supervisors to possess more of the qualities thought to facilitate countertransference management demonstrated better outcomes than did trainees who possessed these qualities to a lesser extent. Although the study did not measure countertransference per se, its findings are consistent with the notion that countertransference behavior interferes with therapeutic goals such that therapists who are better able to manage countertransference have more positive outcomes. Similarly, Rosenberger and Hayes (2002) found indirect evidence for the relationship between countertransference and outcome in that, session by session, therapist management of countertransference was positively related to patient perceptions of the quality of the working alliance. Taken together, data from these studies provide indirect empirical support for the widespread clinical observation that countertransference behavior interferes with outcome. Nonetheless, more research is needed to understand not only the direct relationship between countertransference and outcome but also the complex and subtle ways that therapists' countertransference management abilities mediate this relationship.

It is worth noting that most studies of countertransference behavior have examined the relationship between the frequency of countertransference behavior and some other variables. However, the frequency of a behavior must be distinguished from its impact. For example, several avoidance reactions on the part of the therapist to patient material that the patient considers relatively unimportant may have far less of an effect clinically than the therapist's avoiding, even once, a topic or patient affect that the patient holds to be highly meaningful. Our understanding of countertransference would be advanced considerably if future research accounted for the actual impact of countertransference reactions.

Particular Therapist Characteristics and Behaviors Seem to Facilitate the Management of Countertransference

As discussed in chapter 5, we have conducted work with colleagues to develop and test a theory of countertransference management based on five therapist qualities believed to be important in the regulation of countertransference reactions. These five therapist characteristics are self-insight, anxiety management, empathy, self-integration, and conceptual skills. Together, they comprise the Countertransference Factors Inventory (CFI), an inventory designed for a therapist to be rated by someone familiar with her or his clinical work (e.g., a supervisor or colleague). An initial study found that reputedly excellent therapists were rated higher on all five dimensions of the CFI than therapists in general, supporting the clinical salience of the factors measured by the CFI (Van Wagoner et al., 1991). In addition, psychodynamic therapists were judged to possess better conceptual skills than humanistic therapists; no other characteristics varied as a function of theoretical orientation. In a case study, an experienced therapist's session-by-session self-ratings on the CFI were correlated positively with her patient's ratings of the working alliance and session depth (Rosenberger & Hayes, 2002).

Subsequent research has demonstrated mixed, though generally positive, support for the five specific therapist characteristics that comprise the CFI. Two studies indicated that therapists' conceptual skills are beneficial in managing countertransference, but only when the therapist possesses adequate openness to countertransference feelings (Latts & Gelso, 1995; Robbins & Jolkovski, 1987). When this op
ing, relying purely on theory and conceptualizations appe
ficient for managing countertransference, and may actua
to countertransference behavior. Therapist empathy has
be related inversely to countertransference behavior (Bae

Hayes et al., 1997; Peabody & Gelso, 1982), and positively related to openness to one's countertransference feelings (Peabody & Gelso, 1982). Openness to countertransference feelings, in turn, has been demonstrated to be associated with less countertransference behavior (Robbins & Jolkovski, 1987), although this relationship was not detected in two additional studies (Latts & Gelso, 1995; Peabody & Gelso, 1982). Research also has suggested that therapists who are better self-integrated (i.e., have more stable boundaries, are better differentiated) tend to have fewer countertransference reactions (Gelso et al., 1995; J. A. Hayes et al., 1997; Rosenberger & Hayes, 2002) and more positive outcomes (Gelso et al., 2002). Therapists' ability to manage their anxiety has been found, as one might expect, to reduce their actual countertransference-based anxiety (Gelso et al., 1995), as well as to facilitate client improvement (Gelso et al., 2002).

At present, research has not provided extensive support for the idea that therapist self-insight, in and of itself, is a critical component of countertransference management (Gelso et al., 1995, 2002; J. A. Hayes et al., 1997). This seems more than a little ironic, given the importance attached in the countertransference literature to therapists understanding what is going on inside themselves, affectively, cognitively, and viscerally. One possible explanation is that countertransference researchers have yet to adequately measure therapist self-insight. In one study, for example, therapists' ratings of their self-insight were uncorrelated with supervisors' ratings (J. A. Hayes et al., 1997). It could be that therapists who are more aware of themselves recognize how little they actually know, whereas less self-insightful therapists think that the little they comprehend about themselves is all there is to know. Another possibility is that a more fine-grained analysis of self-insight may be necessary. Self-insight as a trait may be less important than a therapist's moment-to-moment awareness of his or her experience in a given session. In fact, some research suggests that such awareness among therapists may be helpful as long as therapists do not become preoccupied with themselves (Fauth & Williams, 2005; Lesh, 1970; Williams & Fauth, 2005).

On a specific behavioral level, very little research exists that sheds light on what therapists actually do with specific patients to manage their countertransference reactions. During sessions themselves, therapists may use techniques such as thought stopping, self-coaching, breathing, refocusing, and even suppression of affect to deal with countertransference reactions (Baehr, 2004; Williams et al., 1997; Williams, Polster, Grizzard, Rockenbaugh, & Judge, 2003). In between sessions, therapists use peer consultation, their own therapy, and personal reflection to manage countertransference (Baehr, 2004; Williams, Polster, et al., 2003). Therapists also report that self-care activities such as rest, pleasure reading, yoga, and other forms of exercise, as well as scheduling patient appointments within one's limits, made countertransference reactions less likely to occur (Baehr, 2004; Williams, Hurley, O'Brien, & De Gregorio, 2003).

Therapists Should Think Carefully About Disclosing Their Countertransference Reactions, Especially When the Working Alliance Is Not Solid

Self-disclosure may be considered akin to the use of touch in therapy: a double-edged sword that can be either of great benefit or damage, depending upon its use. One of the foremost dangers to therapist self-disclosure is the possibility of role reversal, where the focus of treatment shifts from the patient to the therapist (Matthews, 1988; Widmer, 1995). Therapists also may self-disclose in an attempt to seek validation and approval from the patient, which may undermine the therapy relationship (Wells, 1994). On the whole, however, research indicates that therapist disclosure tends to have favorable effects. Findings from one study suggest that patients especially prefer disclosures that reveal something personal about the therapist (Nilsson, Strassberg, & Bannon, 1979). However, even among those who believe that countertransference can be of therapeutic value, little consensus exists about whether therapists should share with their clients that such reactions have occurred. As Myers and Hayes (2006) note,

> Some writers advocate the judicious use of countertransference disclosures when such revelations might confirm a client's sense of reality, intentionally offset the power imbalance in therapy, foster an authentic therapy relationship, and decrease the client's sense of isolation (Brown, 2001; Gorkin, 1987; J. A. Hayes & Gelso, 2001). Echoing these points is a concerted movement in contemporary analytic thought that advocates for selective self-disclosure by therapists to decrease asymmetry in the therapeutic relationship as a means to make the analytic process more collaborative (Broucek & Ricci, 1998). Renik (1999) and asserts that the traditional notion of analytic anonymity is neither possible nor constructive, and that at times, a therapist's choice to not disclose constrains a dialectical interchange between the client and therapist. Little (1951) takes the extreme perspective of suggesting that if the therapist has exhibited any countertransference behavior, the client should always be made aware of the origins of such behavior. (pp. 175–176)

In their study of the effects of countertransference disclosures (i.e., revelations about therapist areas of unresolved conflict), Myers and Hayes (2006) found that therapists tended to be rated less favorably when countertransference disclosures were made within the context of a weak, working alliance as opposed to a strong working alliance. Sessions were rated as shallower and therapists as less expert in these circumstances. However, when the alliance was strong, countertransference disclosures produced more favorable ratings of the therapist and the session than when no disclosures were made. This finding is consistent with more general research on therapist self-disclosure that indicates that patients tend to view therapist disclosures positively and prefer some therapist disclosure to no therapist disclosure (Hill & Knox, 2002).

Countertransference Reactions Appear to Be Somewhat Infrequent Within Sessions but Relatively Common Across Sessions

Here again it is important to keep in mind the distinction between internal and external countertransference reactions. The cumulative body of research indicates that, within any single session of therapy, displays of countertransference behavior tend to be infrequent. However, research, as well as our own clinical and supervisory observations, suggests that countertransference thoughts and feelings are much more common than overt behavior. Most of the time, these internal reactions are sufficiently managed so that they do not translate into outright displays of countertransference behavior. Stated differently, it would seem that most therapists experience some, but not many, countertransference reactions in most sessions. For example, J. A. Hayes et al. (1998) found in their qualitative investigation of eight experienced therapists that these therapists reported experiencing at least one countertransference reaction, either internal or external, in 80% of their sessions. However, the number of countertransference reactions within any one session was often quite limited. While this finding should be interpreted cautiously due to the limited nature of the sample, it also raises the possibility that the actual occurrence of countertransference reactions was higher. Therapists simply may have been unaware of or unwilling to disclose other instances of countertransference reactions.

One of the implications for ongoing research on countertransference is that infrequently occurring events tend to be assessed with poor reliability. For example, in studying a therapist's overt display of countertransference behavior, if such behavior is exhibited only three times in a session, raters need to catch all three occurrences. If a rater fails to attend to even one display of countertransference behavior, a significant percentage of those behaviors will be missed. From a clinical standpoint, as mentioned earlier, it is important to note that the relative infrequency of countertransference reactions within a session does not diminish their therapeutic significance. As research by Friedman and Gelso (2000) indicates, low amounts of countertransference behavior may be prevalent, but this behavior nonetheless correlates substantially with other relevant therapy variables, including a weakened working alliance (Ligiero & Gelso, 2002).

THE FUTURE OF RESEARCH ON COUNTERTRANSFERENCE

Empirical discoveries related to countertransference are in their beginning stages. The depths of a vast ocean of knowledge remain to be explored. In terms of next steps, there are several areas that we consider to be most important and in need of attention. First, the relationship between countertransference and psychotherapy outcome needs to be better understood. In the nearly one hundred years since Freud first introduced the term countertransference, the number of studies to date that have directly investigated the relationship between countertransference and outcome—one—is woefully insufficient. If it is true, as J. A. Hayes et al. (1997) found, that countertransference behavior is only related to outcome when outcome is below average, then this needs to be substantiated with additional research. Furthermore, the specific pathways by which countertransference reactions interfere with outcome need to be explored and identified. For instance, it could be that countertransference feelings and thoughts, when not successfully managed, lead to countertransference acting out, which could have any number of effects (e.g., ruptures in the working alliance, patients feeling misunderstood by and distrustful of the therapist, decreased patient motivation for therapy). These effects may be the direct contributors to poor outcome.

Second, and equally as important then, additional research is needed that will help therapists understand better how to manage their countertransference reactions. As discussed in chapter 5, this research can take a number of different directions. For example, research efforts are needed to advance our knowledge of how to better prevent harmful countertransference reactions from occurring. How might we help therapists to understand and develop qualities that make it less likely to experience countertransference reactions that are damaging? Given the long-standing emphasis on self insight dating back to Socrates' maxim, "Know thyself," it seems imperative to better understand empirically whether and how self-insight facilitates countertransference management. This seems important both in terms of understanding how self-insight as a trait enhances countertransference management as well as how the therapist's in-session, moment-to-moment awareness of his or her experiences promotes countertransference management. In addition, the five therapist qualities that we have postulated to be related to effective countertransference management represent initial work but they are by no means exhaustive. Further study is needed to understand possible interactions between these variables and to discover other therapist characteristics that might make countertransference reactions less likely to occur. At the same time, research is needed to deepen our knowledge of how therapists can manage their countertransference reactions once they have actually occurred. Especially lacking is research on what therapists can actually do during and between sessions to minimize the negative impact of countertransference reactions. Future research also could profitably investigate the potentially beneficial aspects of countertransference. Theorists and clinicians have long espoused the possible virtues of countertransference, dating back to the origins of the totalistic view (Heimann, 1950; Little, 1951). For example, proponents of the benefits of countertransference have suggested that countertransference can be used to better understand patient dynamics, the therapy relationship, how others might react to the patient, and ideal treatment planning. However, this body of literature offers relatively little in the way of concrete suggestions for how therapists might actually utilize their countertransference reactions to accomplish these aims, and virtually no research has been conducted toward this end either (J. A. Hayes, 2004). This situation needs to be remedied.

Another area in which countertransference research could be quite valuable is in regard to training. In our more than 60 combined years of teaching and supervising therapist trainees, we have experienced myriad challenges of helping students to recognize and deal with their countertransference reactions. Admittedly, we often find ourselves simply doing the best we can, relying on our clinical and supervisory experience, but wishing at times that more formal theory and research existed to guide our efforts. We are often a bit alarmed to read evaluations of trainees' clinical work that describe students, almost in passing, as adept at identifying and handling their countertransference, as if it were easy to do so. Given the complexity of that task, and the fact that the two authors grapple with countertransference consistently in their own clinical work, it is a surprise to know that practicum students are casually described as quite proficient at managing their countertransference reactions. The larger point is this: We know remarkably little about how to effectively train therapists, whether they are novices or seasoned clinicians, about how to identify, process, manage, and make use of countertransference. Research efforts in this direction could be quite fruitful.

To make advances in addressing these and other questions related to countertransference, improvements in research methodology are needed (Hayes, 2004). We need more sophisticated ways of capturing the often-unconscious roots of countertransference reactions. Perhaps future research efforts should borrow from advances that have been made in the realm of projective assessment. It also seems possible to begin to capitalize on knowledge of physiological reactions to stress and use this as a framework for studying countertransference. For example, rather than relying solely on therapist self-report of internal countertransference reactions to patients, it would be helpful to assess physiological indices of therapist reactions to patients (e.g., cortisol levels, autonomic activity). Suffice it to say that continued progress in countertransference research will require creativity on the part of future researchers.

CONCLUSION

We would like to end the chapter by sharing some personal reflections on conducting countertransference research. Although investigating countertransference is challenging for a host of reasons, as noted at the outset of the chapter, it also has been tremendously rewarding and, we hope, of value to therapists and their work with patients. It is our belief, or at least an additional hope, that by contributing to the literature on countertransference, we have helped to destigmatize the construct. That is, by studying countertransference, by attempting to understand it scientifically, we hope that we have contributed to an understanding of countertransference that diminishes its historically taboo nature. Personally, some of the reward of conducting research on countertransference stems from the internal gratification of wrestling with and attempting to overcome the challenges inherent in studying this complex topic. It is, quite simply, intellectually stimulating work. And it is also clinically enriching work. We each have benefited as therapists from studying countertransference. Because the concept often is on our minds, we are more attuned to countertransference in our work with patients than would probably be the case otherwise. Studying countertransference reminds us of our own flaws, our own vulnerabilities, and our own humanity on a regular basis. This not only benefits our clinical work, it enables personal growth as well, in a humbling sort of way. Along the same lines, although we certainly have learned much about countertransference as a result of our studies, we recognize how little we know in relation to what remains to be known. It has also been our experience that conducting research on countertransference has contributed to the clinical supervision we conduct, to the courses we teach, and to our general understanding of therapists, ourselves included.

7

Countertransference and the Psychotherapist's Subjectivity: Conclusions and Recommendations

In this final chapter, we offer a number of conclusions about countertransference and other emotional reactions of the psychotherapist, and how these operate across diverse therapies. The conclusions are offered in the form of statements, which are followed by discussion. Many of these statements reflect material we presented in considerable depth in the preceding chapters. Other statements are amplifications of topics that were touched upon only in a cursory way. Our intent in presenting these statements and discussion is to provide practitioners, researchers, and theoreticians with take-home messages of sorts as they work with and study countertransference and related phenomena.

As you will see, now we summarize what countertransference is and is not; discuss how countertransference and other emotionally based responses of the psychotherapist may be managed in a way that aids rather than hinders treatment; reflect upon the consequences of unmanaged countertransference; and examine patient and therapist factors involved in countertransference feelings and behavior. A theme in this last chapter, as well as in the entire book, is that even when conservatively defined, countertransference is a universal in psychotherapy. It appears frequently, it appears in every theoretical persuasion, and it plays a major role in the psychotherapy process.

1. *Countertransference is Most Fundamentally a Function of the Therapist's Conflicts and Vulnerabilities.* This is perhaps the most basic tenet of our conception of countertransference. Although countertransference may be thought of as a joint creation of patient and therapist (see next section), its most decisive feature is that it is rooted in the therapist. Recall that in chapter 2, we defined countertransference as the therapist's internal or external reactions that are shaped by the therapist's past or present emotional conflicts and vulnerabilities. The therapist's conflicts of which we speak, to one degree of another, must be unresolved for countertransference to happen, especially for it to be acted out in the treatment. In this respect, it will be recalled that we have conceptualized countertransference as occurring at a variety of levels, ranging from exclusively inner experiences of the therapist to behavior that is acted out with the patient (see chap. 2). It is especially in the realm of acted-out behavior that the therapist's unresolved conflicts are involved.

What do we mean by the term *unresolved conflicts?* Here we refer to emotional wounds, conflicts, and what may be referred to as sore points to which the therapist has not found an internal solution. Although these wounds may occur at any point in the therapist's development, they are usually rooted in early childhood. For example, a given therapist may be vulnerable to issues around separation and loss, tied to the fact that her marriage of many years painfully ended a short time ago. This alone could easily make the therapist vulnerable to countertransference with her patients who are dealing with loss issues in relationships. However, unrecognized acting out of countertransference is more likely to occur if this therapist carried unresolved wounds with her from childhood around separation and loss. That is because the early wounds are likely to become part of the self of the therapist, and also are more likely to not be available to consciousness (and thus to conscious control).

The therapist and researcher must also be mindful of the fact that there exist varying degrees of resolution (or lack of it) of the therapist's conflicts. Hopefully, most internal conflicts experienced by the therapist in his or her life are at least mostly resolved. However, even when an emotional conflict is mostly resolved, it may be activated in the treatment hour. For example, a seasoned psychoanalytic therapist may have put most of his issues around being smart enough (which are basically tied to being good enough to be loved by his very smart father) to rest, having come to largely accept who he is, including his level of ability. However, with a certain patient who is very subtly competitive and denigrating, this therapist's mostly resolved issues might get reactivated.

It will be noticed that, in addition to the term *conflict*, we also use the term *vulnerability* in our conception of countertransference. We do so because some countertransference may not be rooted in unresolved conflicts per se, but instead may be part of the therapist's personality structure in a way that makes him or her vulnerable to particular patients. For example, the therapist who is unable to tolerate the intense emotional chaos and the intense oscillation between love and hate exhibited by many patients suffering from borderline personality disorders may be seen as possessing a vulnerability to such patient states. This vulnerability may not reflect an unresolved conflict in the therapist in the sense we have used the term, and may not be rooted in childhood emotional injuries; but the vulnerability still may cause what we consider countertransference, both internally (e.g., excessive anxiety) and behaviorally (e.g., unhelpful responses to the patient tied to the anxiety).

Finally, the concept of countertransference as essentially all of the therapist's emotional reactions to the patient is seen as so broad as to be scientifically and clinically useless (see discussion in chap. 2). Although all of the therapist's emotional reactions are important to the treatment (see chap. 3), not all of them may be usefully considered countertransference. Further, we reject the idea that countertransference reactions are caused by the patient. To be sure, patient reactions do cause therapist reactions, but for the latter to be usefully considered countertransference, there must be a "hook" in the therapist, some conflict or vulnerability that allows the patient's reactions to "get to" the therapist.

2. *Countertransference is Best Understood in Terms of the Countertransference Interaction Hypothesis.* Although the fundamental determinant of countertransference is always the therapist and his or her conflicts and vulnerabilities, we have suggested a decidedly relational perspective on psychotherapy in that the therapeutic relationship and its elements are seen as co-constructed by therapist and patient. *Co-construction* implies that both parties are involved in creating meanings and in the internal and external reactions of each to the other. Thus, although the therapist must have a hook (indicative of unresolved conflict and vulnerability) for countertransference to occur, usually something expressed (verbally or nonverbally) by the patient serves as a precipitant. Such patient triggers touch the therapist in a sore area, and if the therapist is unable to understand or control consciously his or her reactions, countertransference is likely to be acted out.

Having said this, the *Countertransference Interaction Hypothesis* dictates that countertransference results from the interaction of particular patient actions or triggers (words, intimations, characteristics, behaviors) with particular therapist conflicts and vulnerabilities. This hypothesis has been evidenced repeatedly throughout the brief history of empirical research on countertransference. Whereas the efforts to find patient qualities that triggered countertransference in and of themselves have borne little fruit over the years, more complex studies that examined interactions of patient and therapist qualities have made some interesting discoveries. An example derives from the literature on attachment patterns (e.g., John Bowlby's theory of infant and adult attachment) in the therapeutic relationship. Mohr et al. (2005) studied 93 first counseling sessions between clinical and counseling psychology graduate student therapists and their clients. These investigators found that client attachment patterns (fearful, preoccupied, or dismissing patterns) were unrelated to counselor countertransference reactions. However, it was found that "countertransference dynamics were a function of the unique configuration of client and counselor attachment patterns in the therapy dyad" (p. 306). For example, dismissing counselors (in terms of attachment styles) most often displayed countertransference in the form of hostile, critical, and rejecting behaviors with clients who exhibited a preoccupied attachment style. At the same time, counselors with a preoccupied style of attachment displayed this negative pattern with dismissing clients. Similarly, when the client was preoccupied and the therapist was avoidant (high in dismissive and fearful attachment tendencies), the counselors tended to exhibit countertransference in the form of distancing behavior in their sessions. These researchers theorized based on their findings:

> ... an attachment interpretation of such countertransference dynamics is that they result from a pairing in which the client has a relational style that challenges the counselors' own emotion regulation strategies. For example, an avoidant counselor—who would be expected to seek a sense of security by minimizing emotional intensity and interdependence in relationships–might be more likely than others to feel overwhelmed by the exaggerated affect expected in preoccupied clients ... (p. 306)

We should mention that the interactive patterns just described were most prominent when these young therapist trainees had insecure attachment patterns of one kind or another. Also, it was found that therapist trainees who leaned toward the dismissing end of the attachment dimensions tended to exhibit more hostile countertransference with their clients. This suggests an exception to the Countertransference Interaction Hypothesis, and the exception involves what we have termed *chronic countertransference*. Some therapists unfortunately have a pervasive pattern, one that tends to come out with each and every client. Thus, the attachment-dismissive therapist will tend toward hostile countertransference with most or all patients; the "overly helpful" therapist, whose pattern is based on unresolved problems in his or her life, will tend to experience and exhibit countertransference with most or all patients; and the highly competitive therapist will tend to carry his or her conflict-based competitiveness into sessions with most or all clients. Finally, to return to the topic of therapist attachment patterns, the therapist who is securely attached in his or her relationships is much less prone to countertransference, especially what we have referred to as chronic countertransference.

3. *Countertransference Is a Universal Phenomenon in Psychotherapy and Psychoanalysis.* If one takes the totalistic stance regarding countertransference (chap. 1), it naturally follows that countertransference is universal. Because all therapist emotional reactions are countertransferential, and because all therapists have emotional reactions, then it follows that countertransference is a part of all psychotherapy. The problem with this position is that it is uninformative, for, as we have clarified, if countertransference is seen as all therapists' emotional reactions, the concept of countertransference becomes meaningless.

As is clear from the definition of countertransference noted earlier in this chapter and book, we suggest a more conservative and more theoretically nuanced definition. However, even with this definition, we believe that countertransference operates in all psychotherapies, cutting across theories (chap. 3), formats, and durations. Although very limited in quantity, the empirical evidence supports this assertion. The view that countertransference is universal in psychotherapy owes to the fact that by virtue of their humanity, all psychotherapists, no matter how experienced or emotionally healthy, do have unresolved conflicts and vulnerabilities, and that the relational intimacy and emotional demands of psychotherapy tend to exploit those conflicts and vulnerabilities, bringing them into play in the therapeutic work. The best that can be expected is that the psychotherapist is well integrated to the point that the acting out of countertransference is kept to a minimum, and experienced and effective enough to be able to make use of countertransference feelings for the benefit of the work.

Regarding theories, we have shown how countertransference exists importantly in cognitive-behavioral psychotherapy and humanistic-experiential psychotherapy, as well as psychoanalytic treatments, even though the term itself is historically rooted in psychoanalysis. We have pointed out that cognitive-behavior therapists are increasingly examining countertransference phenomena, although they often label it differently. Still, we doubt that cognitive-behavioral therapists will ever pay as much attention to countertransference and other internal states as do, for example, psychodynamic therapists. Nor should they. This is so because the cognitive-behavioral therapist is usefully paying much more attention to other phenomena, for example, the patient's behavioral and cognitive patterns and how to modify these. However, it is important that the cognitive-behavioral therapist heed his or her countertransference reactions, and we suspect that not doing so is the culprit in many failed treatments.

Humanistic therapists, too, often use different terms for what we call countertransference. However, it may not be a simple matter of cognitive-behavioral and humanistic therapists using different terminology. It also may be that these two general theoretical approaches attend less to countertransference than is desirable, as discussed in chapter 3. Our hope is that the material and arguments we have provided facilitate nonanalytic therapists paying closer attention to countertransference than they may have in the past.

4. *Although Countertransference Is Largely Based on Intrapsychic and Interpersonal Phenomena, Cultural Factors Are Often Centrally Involved as Origins and Triggers.* Attention to cultural factors in the practice of psychotherapy has increased dramatically during the past two decades. In the United States, cultural factors have become intertwined with the concept of *oppression* so that reference to culture usually includes minority status in race and/or ethnicity, gender, sexual orientation, socioeconomic status, religion, and physical disability. Within psychotherapy, attention to cultural issues around race and ethnicity has especially burgeoned. However, little has been written about how cultural factors, including race and/or ethnicity, affect and are affected by countertransference.

We offer that cultural factors are usually involved in countertransference, especially when members of the therapeutic dyad are very different culturally, for example, are of different races or sexual orientations. Along this vein, in some cases, countertransference is so tied to cultural factors that it may be seen as either cultural countertransference or culturally reinforced countertransference (Gelso & Mohr, 2001). *Cultural countertransference* (and transference) has been defined by Gelso and Mohr as "culture-related distortions of the patient or rigid interpersonal behaviors rooted in his or her [the therapist's] direct or vicarious experiences with members of the patients RSM [racial/ethnic or sexual minority] group" (p. 59). Each of us carries a template through which we see the world, and this template naturally affects how we see our patients. As regards race and ethnicity, for example, cultural countertransference is operative when the therapist sees his or her patient through the template of the therapist's direct and/or vicarious experience with members of that patient's racial and/or ethnic group. What makes this countertransference is that the therapist may hold onto those perceptions, even as the patient behaves in ways that do not fit. The misperceptions involved in cultural countertransference can seriously undermine the psychotherapy process.

Culturally reinforced countertransference is similar to cultural countertransference, but it has an added feature that we believe makes it even more difficult for the therapist to come to grips with. According to Gelso and Mohr (2001), this added feature is that they are rooted in early childhood experiences. Thus, culturally reinforced countertransference may be seen as culture-related distortions or rigid interpersonal behavior in response to the patient that are connected to and partly stemming from unresolved conflicts with significant others early in the therapist's life. In such countertransference, the cultural component is fueled partly by the earlier roots and partly by the cultural phenomena. An example of culturally reinforced countertransference is the Euro-American therapist who had ambivalent feelings toward his African American patient, where these feelings partly stem from the therapist's perception that people from racial minority groups too often externalize the responsibility for their misfortunes rather than exploring how these misfortunes are determined by intrapsychic factors. Although the ambivalence experienced by the therapist reflected a cultural countertransference, there was more to the story. Deeper exploration revealed that the therapist's perceptions of African Americans and his African American patient were tied to his own difficulties around taking responsibility. This in turn stemmed from exceptional demands he placed upon himself and, further, to a childhood filled with demands. For this therapist to admit responsibility for his own failures would simply be too painful because of the self-criticalness spawned from his childhood. This problem fueled his tendency to overperceive externalization of responsibility, and to react negatively to it when he perceived it. This represents a culturally reinforced countertransference, which this therapist could not resolve until he came to grips with his own conflicts around responsibility and externalization.

Cultural and culturally reinforced countertransferences may operate very subtly. Peggy Rios (in Gelso & Mohr, 2001), a gifted psychotherapist who has considerable experience working with racial and ethnic minority patients, presents an example of subtle countertransference as follows:

> The client was an adolescent Black male. The therapist was a Latina who appeared White. The client presented himself as very angry and was quite challenging and questioning of the therapist in their initial meeting. Thus, he entered therapy with a psychological base of anger that likely had components related to race and gender. The therapist corrected the client's assumption that the therapist couldn't understand his experience as a person of color by telling him that she herself was a Person of Color. She did this because of a countertransference-based need to diffuse the client's anger; but, in doing so, she lost an opportunity to explore affectively his fears about surviving in a

> White world. Rather than acting out her countertransference in this way, the therapist wished she had built an alliance with the client to the point where she could have really dealt in a deep way with his racial issues. Instead she went for a "quick fix" for the strain in the alliance by "coming out" as Latina. (pp. 61–62)

In commenting on this case, Rios noted that had the therapist been a non-Hispanic White person, her defensive reaction to the client's challenge may have been on the order of "Yes, I could never really understand your experience because People of Color have such a hard time of it." Thus, the therapist's cultural countertransference may have been around racial guilt. In both examples, the therapist's fear of potentially alliance-damaging transference (or anger) from the patient stirred a countertransference reaction that, in turn, aimed to foster a quick alliance. Parenthetically, Gelso and Mohr (2001) note that such alliances, which may be termed *premature alliances*, are unlikely to be sound and stable.

5. *Unmanaged Countertransference Tends to Hinder the Process and Outcome of Psychotherapy and Psychoanalysis, and at Times Will Irreparably Damage the Treatment.* In their extensive review of the literature many years ago, B. A. Singer and Luborsky (1977) concluded that:

> *Perhaps the most clear-cut and important area of congruence between the clinical and quantitative literatures is the widely agreed-upon position that uncontrolled countertransference has an adverse effect on therapy outcome.* Not only does it have a markedly detrimental influence on the therapist's technique and interventions, but it also interferes with the optimal understanding of the patient. (p. 449)

Our reviews of the empirical literature (chap. 6, this volume; Gelso & Hayes, 2002; J. A. Hayes & Gelso, 2001), in conjunction with the clinical literature (Gabbard & Lester, 1995; Gelso, 2004) and clinical experience, all come together to support B. A. Singer and Luborsky's (1977) conclusions. As discussed in chapter 6, the empirical literature itself is not conclusive regarding the effects of uncontrolled or unmanaged countertransference on treatment outcome, primarily because there is so very little research on this topic. However, it is very clear that countertransference behavior relates to a host of negative processes during treatment, and it would be very surprising if those negative processes did not in turn relate to negative outcomes. For example, countertransference behavior has been found to relate to a weakened working alliance, and we know from a plethora of research that a weakened alliance is predictive of poorer treatment outcomes (Horvath & Bedi, 2002). So although there is little direct empirical evidence at this point on the effect of what B. A. Singer and Luborsky refer to as "uncontrolled countertransference" on measures of treatment outcome, there is an abundance of indirect empirical evidence, as well as direct clinical evidence.

We should make very clear that our statements about the adverse effects of uncontrolled countertransference pertain to countertransference behavior, or behavior that is acted out in the treatment. Internal countertransference—countertransference-based feelings, thoughts, and visceral sensations–may not have an adverse effect, and indeed may aid the work if the therapist is able to become aware of them and how they relate both to his or her own issues and to what the patient is exhibiting. This is the essence of sound countertransference management (chap. 5, and text to come).

Although the acting out of countertransference during the psychotherapy hour is likely to have a negative impact on the therapeutic relationship and process, we have also noted (chap. 2) that some small "leakage" of countertransference feelings into behavior is probably inevitable and is not harmful if kept to a minimum. In fact, some degree of displaying internal countertransference reactions in the therapist's behavior with the patient may be needed at times for the therapist to become aware that countertransference is occurring. The therapist who notices that he or she is talking too much, taking too much responsibility in the session, being unusually quiet, acting in an aggressive way, or offering advice in a situation in which he or she rarely does so—all of these behaviors may be indicative of internal countertransference and may signal the therapist to look inward to seek an understanding of what he or she is experiencing and what that is about. Such behaviors, and many more, may especially be signaling the existence of internal countertransference when they are accompanied by certain affects. For example, the therapist who has withdrawn his usual level of empathy and is feeling deadened inside, or the therapist who is filling the hour with advice and is also feeling anxiety may both be in the grip of countertransference-based conflict. The combination of behavior that is unusual for the therapist along with internal reactions that are negative in one way or another is an especially important sign that countertransference is operative.

Acting out of countertransference with patients who are particularly provocative is a special case requiring attention. In chapters 1 and 2, we referred to Gabbard's (2001) work with a patient suffering from a borderline personality disorder who was extremely and aggressively provocative with her therapist. In response, and after all else seemed to fail, the therapist did express in a controlled way the frustrated anger he felt, and then he followed this by inviting the patient to explore what had been happening between them. Gabbard viewed such expression as clinically called for, and we agree. The rather mild countertransference behavior allowed him to see more clearly what was transpiring in the treatment, but is also showed the patient that she was dealing with a human being whom she could affect.

Finally, the observations we have made about uncontrolled countertransference and its deleterious effect likely apply to therapies of all theoretical orientations. There is no reason to believe it is more or less harmful in therapies of differing orientations, and it is of great importance that all therapists are on the lookout for the invasion into their work of unmanaged countertransference.

6. *Therapist Self-Insight, Empathy, Self-Integration, Anxiety Management, and Conceptualizing Ability Are Key Constituents of Countertransference Management.* We consider these five factors to be traitlike in the sense that they represent qualities that therapists carry with them in life outside of psychotherapy and also take with them into the session. When these factors are operative within a session, we have theorized that they represent the very elements of countertransference management. For example, the therapist's insight into herself within the therapeutic relationship is a fundamental aspect of her managing her internal countertransference so that it can benefit rather than hinder the work. Similarly, the therapist's actual empathy in the hour is a constituent of managing countertransference in that as he climbs into the patient's world empathically, he is much less likely to be defensively protecting himself from his own anxiety. Regarding self-integration, it is a part of countertransference management in that when the therapist is integrated in the treatment hour with a given patient, and thus has solid but permeable boundaries so that he can differentiate "where he ends and the patient begins" but does not maintain too much distance from the patient–when this happens, countertransference management is occurring, as this self-integration is a key part of such management. Fourth, a key element of countertransference management is the therapist's being able to deal with his or her anxiety, figure out what it is about, and use it to understand the patient. This is what we mean by anxiety management in the context of the therapeutic relationship. As for the fifth factor, conceptualizing ability, the therapist's astuteness in figuring out how the patient's dynamics play into the work and the therapist's experience of the relationship, and how the therapist's and patient's dynamics interplay, is a vital part of countertransference management. Thus, all of the five factors are at play in the treatment hour, and they all are part of how countertransference is managed or mismanaged.

In our initial theorizing about these elements (J. A. Hayes et al., 1991; VanWagoner et al., 1991), we thought of these five elements as factors associated with countertransference management, rather than elements of countertransference management. As our work progressed, we came to realize that these factors were more helpfully considered as constituents of management in that the operation of the factors in the treatment hour represented actually managing countertransference and provided a clue as to just what the therapist needs to be and do to make countertransference work for the therapy rather than against it.

A question with which we have begun to grapple is just how these five key factors interact with one another during the treatment hour. As any therapist knows, the experience of psychotherapy is not neatly divided into factors or elements. Everything is of a piece in that experience exists as an ongoing state. Different qualities of experience come to the fore as the situation demands. Thus, the therapist's empathy for the patient, although hopefully at a high level overall, will wax and wane to an extent, depending upon many factors in each of the participants, as well as their relationship at a given time. Therapist self-insight may emerge as it is called for, and it may work together with empathy in that each influences the other. For example, as a therapist comes to understand that her anxiety with a patient is due to the fact that the patient's pain around losses is pricking at the therapist's wounds in this area, the therapist is freed up to again experience the empathy that had been temporarily lost. Similarly, the therapist's conceptualization of what is occurring between him and the patient, of the dynamics of their interaction, will influence and be influenced by his self-insight, and the two together will interactively affect the therapy process. In statistical terms, we have moderation, mediation, and joint influence. In other words, each of the five factors affects the others; a given factor (e.g., self-integration) may influence treatment process and outcome through its effect on another factor (e.g., anxiety management); and the effect of one of the factors on treatment may depend upon another factor (statistical interaction; see text to come).

The operation of the factor, *conceptualizing ability*, may be special case worth elaborating. In two independent laboratory studies (Latts & Gelso, 1995; Robbins & Jolkovski, 1987) it was found that conceptualizing ability helped therapists control countertransference behavior when the therapist had a sound awareness of his or her countertransference tendencies. However, conceptualizing ability in the absence of such awareness or insight had a negative effect in that therapists were more likely to exhibit countertransference behavior. This is what we meant by a *statistical interaction* in the preceding paragraph.

We conclude this section on countertransference management by suggesting that the empirical and clinical evidence on the importance of the five factors we have theorized is now sufficiently convincing that we believe it important to teach psychotherapist trainees about these factors and their importance in countertransference management. How to best do this is a question worth the attention of psychotherapy trainers in the years ahead.

7. *The Therapist's Psychological Wounds That Are Sufficiently Healed, and Conflicts That Are Sufficiently Resolved, Can Facilitate the Psychotherapy Pro-*

cess. In chapter 5, we discussed the Wounded Healer metaphor in some depth. The basic point of this metaphor is that by virtue of our humanity, we therapists all must have conflicts and emotional wounds. During childhood, the inevitable wounds of growing up become melded into our personalities and identities, some becoming largely resolved, others "worked around" so that we can live our lives mostly without their impediment, and still others affecting much of what we do. Those who seek to become psychotherapists certainly seem to have their share of these wounds and conflicts, and probably have a sharper awareness of them than do others. Professional training in psychotherapy, personal psychotherapy, and maturity all facilitate the growing therapist's resolution of these wounds and conflicts. However, the resolution is never complete; and, to one degree or another, our vulnerabilities are susceptible to the patient's revelations and projections during the treatment process. We are all wounded healers.

At the same time, the very fact that we have wounds is part and parcel of our ability to help others. Why is this so? The wounds, and the experiences that formed them, foster in the therapist a first-hand understanding, sensitivity, and motivation to help. They also facilitate humility in the therapist, a sense that in a deeply important way, therapist and patient are fellow travelers in the journey of life. The great existential psychotherapist, Irving Yalom (2002) captures these concepts nicely, as follows:

> ... I prefer to think of my patients and myself as *fellow travelers*, a term that abolishes the distinction between "them" (the afflicted) and "us" (the healers). During my training I was often exposed to the idea of the fully analyzed therapist, but as I progressed through life, formed intimate relationships with a good many of my therapist colleagues, met the senior figures in the field, been called upon to render help to my former therapists and teachers, and myself become a teacher and an elder, I have come to realize the mythic nature of this idea. We are all in this together and there is no therapist and no person immune to the inherent tragedies of existence. (p. 8)

The qualities we have noted are part of the therapist's empathic attunement with patients, and they also provide the therapist with knowledge about emotional conflict in general. However, if this personal experience with suffering is to allow for the wise use of countertransference rather than simply acting out one's psychological conflicts in the treatment, the wounds need to be at least mostly healed, or at least understood enough to prevent them from infecting the work and the therapeutic relationship.

We have noted at several points in this book the fact that the theoretical and empirical literatures on countertransference focus a great deal on the negative possibilities, on how the acting out of countertransference can be damaging to the treatment. Relatively little has been devoted to the questions of just how and why countertransference can facilitate the therapeutic process. To summarize our answer, regarding the "how" question first, when material in the therapy (e.g., the patient's verbal or nonverbal expressions) touches the therapist in a vulnerable place, the therapist experiences feelings, thoughts or sensations (or exhibits behaviors) that are "off-center" enough to serve as a cue that something is awry. This is also a cue to look inward to understand just what is being stirred in the therapist, what in the patient is causing the reaction, and how this relates to the patient's internal dynamics and what he or she typically stirs in others. As to the "why" question, the very fact that the therapist has unresolved conflicts and vulnerabilities provides the therapist with the kind of sensitivities to the patient's expressions and projections that then foster the therapist's quest to understand what is being stirred in him or her, why it is being stirred, and what this has to do with the patient's dynamics and core issues. However, as we have said, if the wounds are too great, not sufficiently healed, and/or not sufficiently understood, these same sensitivities may just cause the therapist to act out his or her countertransference. When this happens, patient and therapist are no longer fellow travelers.

8. *The Inner World of the Psychotherapist, Including Noncountertransference Elements, Is a Vital Element of all Psychotherapies.* As discussed in detail in chapter 4, there is a large portion of the therapist's inner world that is not captured by the concept of countertransference. The therapist's inner experience that is free from unresolved conflicts and vulnerabilities comes into play in psychotherapy. Indeed, it is tremendously important that the therapist be able to experience the range of inner experience during the therapy. For example, the good therapist feels, and at times, he or she feels a lot. And, as we have said, very often these feelings are not countertransference based. This inner world is a vital part of psychotherapy of any theoretical orientation.

Much of the therapist's inner experience will directly benefit the patient. For example, the therapist's experience of empathy, liking, appreciation, concern, and even nonerotic loving are very likely to be facilitative of the patient's growth. Even more negative noncountertransference feelings will turn out to be facilitative when they are experienced in the context of a caring relationship and when they are used in a well-timed and sensitive manner to help the patient understand how he or she affects others.

The interplay of countertransference and noncountertransference reactions is one of the key elements of psychotherapy, but one that has been infrequently addressed over the years. So often, the therapist's inner reaction is some combination of countertransference and feelings that are not countertransference based. For example, when the therapist quietly seethes in response to his obsessive patient's frequent criticisms of his empathic responses, part of what the therapist feels is an almost inevitable human response that this patient so frequently elicits in others. However, another part of the therapist's inner response to the patient's criticisms is tied to this therapist's feeling that he could never be enough for his hypercritical, alcoholic father. So this therapist has considerable vulnerability to attacks of his therapy skills from hypercritical patients.

It has been our experience based on clinical supervision and our own work as therapists that what may seem like a purely normal reaction to difficult patients hides the more subtle countertransference part of this reaction. Of course, we have worked with therapy trainees who seemed intent on taking total responsibility for all of their less-than-desirable reactions to patients, thus missing the strong pull from the patient for those reactions, and at times the hidden intent of the patient to stir these reactions.

Therapists of all theoretical persuasions of course have inner experiences such as feelings, thoughts, images, and the like. And it is important for therapists of all orientations to both be aware of this inner experience and consider if and how it may be used for the benefit of the patient. As we discussed in chapter 4, even the less affect-oriented therapies such as cognitive-behavior therapy are now paying more attention to what the therapist experiences in the hour.

9. *We Now Have the Beginnings of an Empirically Based Understanding of Countertransference, but Continued Research From all Methodological Vantage Points Is Needed.* Although a sizeable body of clinical and theoretical literature on countertransference has developed over the years, research has lagged behind. This lag is likely due to the fact that countertransference is a highly elusive construct, one that does not lend itself readily to scientific study. Any construct that implicates so centrally unconscious processes in the therapist is going to be hard to investigate, but when those processes are also experienced as shameful and even antitherapeutic, research at times seems impossible. Despite these fundamental difficulties, research has indeed progressed, especially during the past two decades. In fact, we can no longer say that research on countertransference is in its infancy. *Adolescence* may be a more apt term, because countertransference research has grown to the point of having an identity within the broad field of psychotherapy research, albeit an identity that is often unclear and at times a bit confused. As can be seen in chapter 6, important and clinically meaningful findings have emerged over the years. Rather than repeat those findings in this chapter, we would like instead to comment further on methodological requirements and some key research needs on the topic.

Regarding methodology, many of the studies that have been conducted on countertransference have occurred in the psychology laboratory, and have been simulations of actual treatment rather than treatment itself. Although one always wonders about the real-life implications of such research (the external validity), analogue research can be uniquely useful to the study of processes that are hard or even impossible to study outside of the laboratory. In the laboratory we can have greater control of variables and also can manipulate variables that it would be unethical to manipulate in the field. For example, we can randomly assign therapists to respond to videotaped actresses playing the role of lesbian, gay, or heterosexual clients (Gelso et al., 1995; J. A. Hayes & Gelso, 1993); study therapists' countertransference reactions to videotaped client actresses playing the role of a patient who had recently been date raped (Latts & Gelso, 1995); examine how therapists' discomfort with anger influences their countertransference reactions to a videotaped angry client actor exhibiting anger toward her therapist (Sharkin & Gelso, 1993). Each of these studies sheds light on countertransference phenomena, and none of them could have been done in the field.

We are at a time in the history of psychotherapy research in which intellectual pragmatism is at a peak. There is a tendency to value only studies that have direct clinical relevance. Thus, the highest esteem is placed on controlled outcome studies done in the field. Some clinical journals even have had a policy against publishing laboratory research. In our view, this kind of pragmatism represents a shortsighted view of science, a view that dictates immediate results at the expense of the kind of long-term understanding that comes from piecing together findings derived from a range of methodological approaches. What is most needed in the area of countertransference research is methodological diversity, in which the topic is empirically attacked in a variety of ways with diverse methods.

Methodologically, the new kid on the block is qualitative research, an approach that seeks to understand deeply the therapist's own view of the questions being addressed. Such research typically involves intensely interviewing a small number of therapists. Although traditional researchers who are steeped in the kind of pragmatism we have noted tend to eschew qualitative research, we believe it is an extremely useful approach that, like laboratory analogue studies, is capable of answering questions that traditional quantitative studies cannot. For example, in-depth interviews with therapists can reveal what countertransference problems they experience with their patients and how they addressed those problems (Gelso et al., 1999; J. A. Hayes et al., 1998; Hill et al., 1996; Williams et al., 1997).

Finally, small sample quantitative studies can also be illuminating. The classic study by Cutler (1958), for example, examined countertransference in only two therapist trainees, and the findings were of great heuristic value, suggesting that when patients touched on personally conflictual topics, therapists tended to report their own and their patients' behavior inaccurately. More recently, Rosenberger and Hayes

(2002) studied a single dyad for 13 sessions and, found that when the therapist's personal issues were touched upon, the therapist tended to rate herself as less expert, attractive, and trustworthy; and she judged the sessions to be shallower.

Although the three kinds of studies we have mentioned (laboratory analogues, qualitative research, and small sample quantitative research) all have their own unique limitations, each can add usefully to more traditional methods in helping us learn about and understand countertransference. The use of a range of methods to study phenomena is often referred to as *methodological triangulation*. Such triangulation has occurred in the area of countertransference research, and our call is for continued triangulation.

In chapter 6, we pointed to countertransference topics in greatest need of research. We would like to close this treatment of countertransference by underscoring our belief that the greatest need is for more research and, in particular, more programs of research on this topic that had been avoided for decades but is vital to the practice of effective psychotherapy.

CONCLUSION

The being and subjectivity of the psychotherapist are fundamental and vital elements of psychotherapy from every theoretical position, and countertransference is a central part of that subjectivity. Although the concept of countertransference has had a shaky history, it is now coming into its own as a key universal and transtheoretical construct. It has been a thesis of this book that each and every psychotherapist experiences countertransference internally and that we all exhibit countertransference-based behavior to one degree or another. Countertransference, and indeed all the therapist's subjectivity, can be for better or worse. If left unattended it can literally destroy the treatment, whereas if understood and used wisely, countertransference can be perhaps the therapist's most powerful and trustworthy source. We can avoid facing countertransference or we can seek to bring it into the treatment process, but we cannot make it go away through neglect or indifference. From this perspective, the choice is simple, but the process deeply complex.

References

Anchin, J. C., & Kiesler, D. J. (1982). *Handbook of interpersonal psychotherapy*. Elmsford, NY: Pergamon.
Anderson, S. C., & Mandell, D. L. (1989). The use of self-disclosure by professional social workers. *Social Casework: The Journal of Contemporary Social Casework, 70,* 259–267.
Aron, L. (1991). The patient's experience of the analyst's subjectivity. *Psychoanalytic Dialogues, 1,* 29–51.
Aron, L. (1996). *A meeting of minds: Mutuality and psychoanalysis.* Hillsdale, NJ: Analytic Press.
Assagioli, R. (1965). *Psychosynthesis*. New York: Penguin.
Baehr, A. P. (2004). *Wounded healers and relational experts: A grounded theory of experienced psychotherapists' management and use of countertransference*. Unpublished doctoral thesis, Pennsylvania State University.
Bandura, A., Lipsher, D. H., & Miller, P. E. (1960). Psychotherapists' approach-avoidance reactions to patients' expressions of hostility. *Journal of Consulting Psychology, 24,* 1–8.
Barrett-Lennard, G. T. (1981). The empathy cycle: Refinement of a nuclear concept. *Journal of Counseling Psychology, 28,* 91–100.
Beck, A. T., Rush, A. J., Shaw, B. F., & Emery, G. (1979). *Cognitive therapy of depression*. New York: Guilford.
Beck, J. S. (1996). Cognitive therapy of personality disorders. In P. M. Salkovskis (Ed.), *Frontiers of cognitive therapy* (pp. 165–181). New York: Guilford.
Beres, D., & Arlow, J. A. (1974). Fantasy and identification in empathy. *Psychiatric Quarterly, 43,* 26–50.
Bly, R. (1988). *A little book on the human shadow.* New York: HarperCollins.
Bohart, A. C. (2002). How does the relationship facilitate productive client thinking? *Journal of Contemporary Psychotherapy, 32,* 61–69.
Bohart, A. C., Elliott, R., Greenberg, L. S., & Watson, J. C. (2002). Empathy. In J. C. Norcross (Ed.), *Psychotherapy relationships that work* (pp. 89–108). New York: Oxford University Press.

Boyer, S. P., & Hoffman, M. A. (1993). Counselor affective reactions to termiantion: Impact of counselor loss history and perceived client sensitivity to loss. *Journal of Counseling Psychology*, *40*, 271–277.
Broucek, F., & Ricci, W. (1998). Self-disclosure or self presence? *Bulletin of the Menninger Clinic*, *62*, 427–438.
Brown, L. S. (2001). Feelings in context: Countertransference and the real world in feminist therapy. *Journal of Clinical Psychology/In Session*, *57*, 1005–1012.
Bugental, J. F. T. (1978). *Psychotherapy and process*. New York: Random House.
Butler, S. F., Flasher, L. V., & Strupp, H. H. (1993). Countertransference and qualities of the psychotherapist. In N. E. Miller, L. Luborsky, J. P. Barber, & J. P. Docherty (Eds.), *Psychodynamic treatment research: A handbook for clinical practice* (pp. 342–359). New York: Basic Books.
Castonguay, L. G., & Hill, C. E. (Eds.). (2006). *Insight in psychotherapy*. New York: Guilford.
Coen, S. J. (2000). Why we need to write openly about our clinical cases. *Journal of the Psychoanalytic Association*, *48*(2), 449–470.
Cohen, M. B. (1952). Countertransference and anxiety. *Psychiatry*, *15*, 231–245.
Corsini, R. J. (1999). *Dictionary of psychology*. Philadelphia: Brunner/Mazel.
Crowley, R. M. (1950). Human reactions of analysts to patients. In B. Wolstein (Ed.), *Essential papers on countertransference* (pp. 84–90). New York: New York University Press.
Cruz, J., & Hayes, J. A. (2006, June). *Countertransference in termination: Therapist loss resolution and fear of intimacy*. Paper presented at the North American Society for Psychotherapy Research Conference, Burr Oak, Ohio.
Culbreth, J. R. (2000). Substance abuse counselors with and without a personal history of chemical dependency: A review of the literature. *Alcoholism Treatment Quarterly*, *18*, 67–82.
Curtis, J. M. (1981). Indications and contra-indications in the use of therapist's self-disclosure. *Psychology Reports*, *49*, 499–507.
Cutler, R. L. (1958). Countertransference effects in psychotherapy. *Journal of Consulting Psychotherapy*, *22*, 349–356.
Dowd, E. T., & Courchaine, K. E. (1996). Implicit learning, tacit knowledge, and implications for stasis and change in cognitive psychotherapy. *Journal of Cognitive Psychotherapy*, *10*, 163–180.
Eagle, M. N. (2000). A critical evaluation of current conceptions of transference and countertransference. *Psychoanalytic Psychology*, *17*, 24–37.
Eagle, M. N. (2003). The postmodern turn in psychoanalysis: A critique. *Psychoanalytic Psychology*, *20*, 411–424.
Edwards, C. E., & Murdock, N. L. (1994). Characteristics of therapist self-disclosure in the counseling process. *Journal of Counseling and Development*, *72*, 384–389.
Ellis, A. (2001). Rational and irrational aspects of countertransference. *Journal of Clinical Psychology/In Session*, *57*, 999–1004.
Epstein, L., & Feiner, A. H. (Eds.). (1979). *Countertransference*. New York: Aronson.
Epstein, L., & Feiner, A. H. (1988). Countertransference: The therapist's contribution to treatment. In B. Wolstein (Ed.), *Essential papers on countertransference* (pp. 282–303). New York: New York University Press.
Evans, F. B. III (1996). *Harry Stack Sullivan: Interpersonal theory and psychotherapy*. New York: Routledge.
Fauth, J., & Hayes, J. A. (2006). Counselors' stress appraisals as predictors of countertransference behavior with male clients. *Journal of Counseling and Development*, *84*, 430–439.
Fauth, J., & Williams, E. N. (2005). The in-session self-awareness of therapist-trainees: Hindering or helpful? *Journal of Counseling Psychology*, *52*, 443–447.

Feldman, M. (1997). Projective identification: The analyst's involvement. *International Journal of Psychoanalysis, 78,* 227–241.

Fenichel, O. (1940). *Problems of psychoanalytic technique*. Albany, NY: Psychoanalytic Quarterly, Inc.

Ferenzi, S., & Rank, O. (1923). The development of psychoanalysis. New York: Dover Publications.

Fiedler, F. E. (1951). A method of objective quantification of certain countertransference attitudes. *Journal of Clinical Psychology, 7,* 101–107.

Freud, S. (1959). Future prospects of psychoanalytic psychotherapy. In J. Strachey (Ed. & Trans.), *The standard edition of the complete psychological works of Sigmund Freud* (Vol. 11, pp. 139–151). London: Hogarth Press. (Original work published 1910)

Freud, S. (1959a). The dynamics of transference. In J. Riviere (Ed. & Trans.), *Collected papers of Sigmund Freud* (Vol. 2, pp. 312–322). (Original work published in 1912)

Freud, S. (1959b). Recommendations for physicians on the psycho-analytic method of treatment. In J. Riviere (Ed. & Trans.), *Collected papers of Sigmund Freud* (Vol. 2, pp. 323–341). (Original work published in 1912)

Freud, S. (1959). Inhibitions, symptoms, and anxiety. In J. Strachey (Ed. and Trans.), *The standard edition of the complete psychological works of Sigmund Freud*. (Vol. 20, pp. 87–172). London: Hogarth. (Original work published 1926)

Friedman, S., & Gelso, C. J. (2000). The development of the Inventory of Countertransference Behavior. *Journal of Clinical Psychology, 56,* 1221–1235.

Fromm-Reichmann, F. (1950). *Principles of intensive psychotherapy.* Chicago: University of Chicago Press.

Gabbard, G. O. (2001). A contemporary model of countertransference. *Journal of Clinical Psychology, 58,* 861–867.

Gabbard, G. O., & Lester, E. P. (1995). *Boundaries and boundary violations in psychoanalysis*. Washington, DC: American Psychiatric Press.

Gabbard, G. O., & Wilkinson, S. M. (2000). *Management of countertransference with borderline patients*. Washington, DC: American Psychiatric Press.

Gelso, C. J. (2004). Countertransference and its management in brief dynamic therapy. In D. P. Charman (Ed.), *Core processes in brief psychodynamic psychotherapy* (pp. 231–250). Mahwah, NJ: Lawrence Erlbaum Associates.

Gelso, C. J. (2006). Applying theories to research: The interplay of theory and research in science. In F. Leong & J. Austin (Eds.), *Psychology research handbook: A primer for graduate students and research assistants* (2nd ed., pp. 455–464). Thousand Oaks, CA: Sage.

Gelso, C. J., Fassinger, R. E., Gomez, M. J., & Latts, M. G. (1995). Countertransference reactions to lesbian clients: The role of homophobia, counselor gender, and countertransference management. *Journal of Counseling Psychology, 42,* 356–364.

Gelso, C. J., & Hayes, J. A. (1998). *The psychotherapy relationship: Theory, research, and practice.* New York: Wiley.

Gelso, C. J., & Hayes, J. A. (2002). The management of countertransference. In J. Norcross (Ed.), *Psychotherapy relationships that work* (pp. 267–284). New York: Oxford University Press.

Gelso, C. J., Hill, C. E., Mohr, J. J., Rochlen, A. B., & Zack, J. (1999). Describing the face of transference: Psychodynamic therapists' recollections about transference in cases of successful long-term therapy. *Journal of Counseling Psychology, 46,* 257–267.

Gelso, C. J., Latts, M. G., Gomez, M. J., & Fassinger, R. E. (2002). Countertransference management and therapy outcome: An initial evaluation. *Journal of Clinical Psychology, 58,* 861–867.

Gelso, C. J., & Mohr, J. J. (2001). The working alliance and the transference/countertransference relationship: Their manifestation with racial/ethnic and sexual orientation minority clients and therapists. *Applied and Preventive Psychology, 10,* 51–68.

Glover, E. (1927). Lectures on technique in psycho-analysis. *International Journal of Psycho-analysis, 8,* 311–338, 486–520.

Goldfried, M. R., & Davidson, G. C. (1982). *Clinical behavior therapy.* New York: Wiley.

Goldfried, M. R., & Davila, J. (2005). The role of relationships and technique in therapeutic change. *Psychotherapy: Theory, Research, Practice, and Training, 42,* 421–430.

Gorkin, M. (1987). *The uses of countertransference.* Northvale, NJ: Jason Aronson.

Greenberg, J. R. (1991). Countertransference and reality. *Psychoanalytic Dialogues, 1,* 52–73.

Greenberg, J. R., & Mitchell, S. A. (1983). Object relations in psychoanalytic theory. Cambridge, MA: Harvard University Press.

Greenberg, L. S. (2002). *Emotion-focused therapy: Coaching clients to work through their feelings.* Washington, DC: American Psychological Association.

Greenberg, L. S., Rice, L. N., & Elliott, R. (1993). *Facilitating emotional change.* New York: Guilford.

Greenson, R. R. (1960). Empathy and its vicissitudes. *International Journal of Psychoanalysis, 41,* 418–424.

Greenson, R. R. (1974). Loving, hating, and indifference toward the patient. In R. R. Greenson (Ed.), *Explorations in psychoanalysis* (pp. 505–518). New York: International Universities Press.

Guggenbuhl-Craig, A. (1971). *Power in the helping professions.* Zurich: Spring.

Gurdjieff, G. I. (1973). *Views from the real world.* New York: Penguin.

Halifax, J. (1982). *Shaman: The wounded healer.* New York: Crossroad.

Hatcher, S. L., Favorite, T. K., Hardy, E. A., Goode, R. L., DeShetler, L. A., & Thomas R. M. (2005). An analogue study of therapist empathic process: Working with difference. *Psychotherapy, 42,* 198–210.

Hayes, J. A. (1995). Countertransference in group psychotherapy: Waking a sleeping dog. *International Journal of Group Psychotherapy, 45,* 521–535.

Hayes, J. A. (2004). The inner world of the psychotherapist: A program of research on countertransference. *Psychotherapy Research, 14,* 21–36.

Hayes, J. A., & Gelso, C. J. (1991). Effects of therapist trainees' anxiety and empathy on countertransference behavior. *Journal of Clinical Psychology, 47,* 284–290.

Hayes, J. A., & Gelso, C. J. (1993). Male counselors' discomfort with gay and HIV-infected clients. *Journal of Counseling Psychology, 40,* 86–93.

Hayes, J. A., & Gelso, C. J. (2001). Clinical implications of research on countertransference: Science informing practice. *Journal of Clinical Psychology/In Session, 57,* 1041–1051.

Hayes, J. A., Gelso, C. J., Van Wagoner, S. L., & Diemer, R. A. (1991). Managing countertransference: What the experts think. *Psychological Reports, 69,* 139–148.

Hayes, J. A., McCracken, J. E., McClanahan, M. K., Hill, C. E., Harp, J. S., & Carozzoni, P. (1998). Therapist perspectives on countertransference: Qualitative data in search of a theory. *Journal of Counseling Psychology, 45,* 468–482.

Hayes, J. A., Riker, J. R., & Ingram, K. M. (1997). Countertransference behavior and management in brief counseling: A field study. *Psychotherapy Research, 7,* 145–153.

Hayes, S. C., Strosahl, K. D., & Wilson, K. (1999). *Acceptance and commitment therapy: An experiential approach to behavior change.* New York: Guilford.

Heimann, P. (1950). Countertransference. *British Journal of Medical Psychology, 33,* 9–15.

Hill, C. E., & Knox, S. (2002). Self-disclosure. In J. C. Norcross (Ed.), *Psychotherapy relationships that work* (pp. 255–265). New York: Oxford University Press.

Hill, C. E., Nutt-Williams, E., Heaton, K. J., Thompson, B. J., & Rhodes, R. H. (1996). Therapist retrospective recall of impasses in long-term psychotherapy: A qualitative analysis. *Journal of Counseling Psychology, 43*, 207–217.

Holtforth, M. G., & Castonguay, L. G. (2005). Relationship and techniques in cognitive-behavioral therapy: A motivational approach. *Psychotherapy, 42*, 443–455.

Horney, K. (1939). *New ways in psychoanalysis*. New York: Norton.

Horvath, A. O., & Bedi, R. P. (2002). The alliance. In J. C. Norcross (Ed.), *Psychotherapy relationships that work* (pp. 37–69). New York: Oxford University Press.

Jackson, S. W. (2001). The wounded healer. *Bulletin of the History of Medicine, 75*, 1–36.

Jacobs, T. J. (1991). *The use of the self: Countertransference and communication in the analytic situation*. Madison, CT: International Universities Press.

Jacobs, T. J. (1997). Some reflections on the question of self-disclosure. *Psychotherapy, 26*, 290–295.

Jacobs, T. J. (1999). On the question of self-disclosure by the analyst: Error or advance in technique? *Psychoanalytic Quarterly*, 68, 159–183.

Jourard, S. M. (1971). *The transparent self*. New York: Van Nostrand Reinhold.

Jung, C. G. (1963). *Memories, dreams, reflections*. New York: Random House.

Kabat-Zinn, J. (2003). Mindfulness-based interventions in context: Past, present, and future. *Clinical Psychology: Science and Practice, 10*, 144–156.

Kaslow, F. W. (2001). Whither countertransference in couples and family therapy: A systemic perspective. *Journal of Clinical Psychology/In Session, 57*,1029–1040

Kernberg, O. (1965). Notes on countertransference. *Journal of the American Psychoanalytic Association, 13*, 38–56.

Kernberg, O. (1975). *Borderline states and pathological narcissism*. New York: Aronson.

Kernberg, O. (1976). *Object relations theory and clinical psychoanalysis*. New York: Jason Aronson.

Kiesler, D. J. (1996). Contemporary interpersonal theory and research: *Personality, psychopathology, and psychotherapy*. New York: Wiley.

Kiesler, D. J. (2001). Therapist countertransference: In search of common themes and empirical referents. *Journal of Clinical Psychology/In Session, 57*, 1053–1063.

Klein, M. (1946). Notes on some schizoid mechanisms. *International Journal of Psychoanalysis, 27*, 433–438.

Klein, M. (1975). On identification. In *Envy and gratitude and other works, 1946–1963* (pp. 141–175). New York, NY: Delacorte Press/Seymour Lawrence. (Original work published 1955)

Kohlenberg, R. J., & Tsai, M. (1995). Functional analytic psychotherapy: A behavioral approach to intensive treatment. In W. T. O'Donohue & L. Krasner (Eds.), *Theories of behavior therapy: Exploring behavior change* (pp. 637–658). Washington, DC: American Psychological Association.

Kohut, H. (1959). Introspection, empathy, and psychoanalysis: An examination of the relationship between mode of observation and theory. *Journal of the American Psychoanalytic Association*, 7, 459–483.

Kohut, H. (1977). *The restoration of the self*. New York: International Universities Press.

Kohut, H. (1984). *How does analysis cure?* Chicago: University of Chicago Press.

Kris, E. (1950). On preconscious mental processes. *Psychoanalytic Quarterly, 19*, 540–560.

Lambert, M. J., & Barley, D. E. (2002). Research summary on the therapeutic relationship and psychotherapy outcome. In J. C. Norcross (Ed.), *Psychotherapy relationships that work* (pp. 17–32). New York: Oxford University Press.

Lambert, M. J., & Ogles, B. M. (2004). The efficacy and effectiveness of psychotherapy. In M. J. Lambert (Ed.), *Handbook of psychotherapy and behavior change* (5th ed., pp. 139–193). New York: Wiley.

Lang, P. J., Melamed, B. G., & Hart, J. (1970). A psychophysiological analysis of fear modification using an automated desensitization procedure. *Journal of Abnormal Psychology, 76,* 220–234.

Laskowski, C., & Pellicore, K. (2002). The wounded healer archetype: Applications to palliative care practice. *American Journal of Hospice and Palliative Care, 19,* 403–407.

Latts, M. G., & Gelso, C. J. (1995). Countertransference behavior and management with survivors of sexual assault. *Psychotherapy 32,* 405–415.

Layden, M. A., Newman, C. F., Freeman, A., & Morse, S. B. (1993). *Cognitive therapy of borderline personality disorder.* Needham Heights, MA: Allyn & Bacon.

Lecours, S., Bouchard, M. A., & Normandin, L. (1995). Countertransference as the therapists' mental activity: Experience and gender differences among psychoanalytically oriented psychologists. *Psychoanalytic Psychology, 12,* 259–279.

Lejuez, C. W., Hopko, D. R., Levine, S., Gholkar, R., & Collins, L. M. (2005). The therapeutic alliance in behavior therapy. *Psychotherapy, 42,* 456–468.

Lesh, T. V. (1970). Zen meditation and the development of empathy in counselors. *Journal of Humanistic Psychology, 10,* 39–74.

Levenson, H. (1995). *Time-limited dynamic psychotherapy.* New York: Basic Books.

Ligiero, D. P., & Gelso, C. J. (2002). Countertransference, attachment, and the working alliance: The therapist's contribution. *Psychotherapy, 39,* 3–11.

Linehan, M. M. (1993). *Cognitive behavioral treatment of borderline personality disorder.* New York: Guilford Press.

Little, M. (1951). Countertransference and the patients' response to it. *International Journal of Psychoanalysis, 32,* 32–40.

Little, M. (1957). "R"—The analyst's response to his patient's needs. *International Journal of Psychoanalysis, 58,* 365–374.

Luborsky, L., & Crits-Christoph, P. (1990). *Understanding transferences.* New York: Basic Books.

Maeder, T. (1989). *Children of psychiatrists and other psychotherapists.* New York: Harper & Row.

Mahrer, A. R. (1986). *Therapeutic experiencing: The process of change.* New York: Norton.

Mahrer, A. R. (2001). An experiential alternative to countertransference. *Journal of Clinical Psychology/In Session, 57,* 1021–1028.

Mahrer, A. R., Boulet, D. B., & Fairweather, D. R. (1994). Beyond empathy: Advances in the clinical theory and methods of empathy. *Clinical Psychology Review, 14,* 183–198.

Maltsberger, J. T., & Buie, D. H. (1989). Common errors in the management of suicidal patients. In D. Jacobs & H. N. Brown (Eds.), *Suicide* (pp. 285–294). Madison, CT: International Universities Press.

Maroda, K. (1991). *The power of countertransference.* New York: Wiley.

Maslow, A. H. (1968). *Toward a psychology of being.* New York: Van Nostrand.

Matthews, B. (1988). The role of therapist self-disclosure in psychotherapy: A survey of therapists. *American Journal of Psychotherapy, 42,* 521–531.

McClure, B. A., & Hodge, R. W. (1987). Measuring countertransference and attitude in therapeutic relationships. *Psychotherapy, 24,* 325–335.

McGoldrick, M., Giordano, J., & Pearce, J. K. (Eds.). (1996). *Ethnicity and family therapy.* New York: Guilford.

Mitchell, S. A. (1988). *Relational concepts in psychoanalysis.* Cambridge, MA: Harvard University Press.

Mitchell, S. A. (1997). *Influence and autonomy in psychoanalysis.* Hillsdale, NJ: Analytic Press.

Mitchell, S. A., & Aron, L. (1999). (Eds.) *Relational psychoanalysis.* Hillsdale, NJ: Analytic Press.

Mohr, J. J., Gelso, C. J., & Hill, C. E. (2005). Client and counselor trainee attachment as predictors of session evaluation and countertransference behavior in first counseling sessions. *Journal of Counseling Psychology, 52*, 298–309.

Myers, D., & Hayes, J. A. (2006). Effects of therapist general self-disclosure and countertransference disclosure on ratings of the therapist and session. *Psychotherapy, 43*, 173–185..

Najavits, L. M., & Weiss, R. D. (1994). Variations in therapist effectiveness in the treatment of patients with substance use disorders: An empirical review. *Addiction, 89*, 679–688.

Nilsson, D. E., Strassberg, D. S., & Bannon, J. (1979). Perceptions of counselor self-disclosure: An analogue study. *Journal of Counseling Psychology, 26*, 399–404.

Norcross, J. C. (Ed.). (2001). Empirically supported therapy relationships: Summary of the Division 29 Task Force [Special Issue]. *Psychotherapy, 38*.

Normandin, L., & Bouchard, M. A. (1993). The effects of theoretical orientation and experience on rational, reactive, and reflective countertransference. *Psychotherapy Research, 3*, 77–94.

Nouwen, H. J. M. (1972). *The wounded healer.* New York: Doubleday.

Ogden, T. H. (1982). *Projective identification and therapeutic technique.* New York: Jason Aronson.

Ogden, T. H. (1994). *Subjects of analysis.* New York: Jason Aronson.

Orr, D. (1954). Transference and countertransference: A historical survey. *Journal of the American Psychoanalytic Association, 2*, 621–670.

Ouspensky, P. D. (1949). *In search of the miraculous.* New York: Random House.

Peabody, S. A., & Gelso, C. J. (1982). Countertransference and empathy: The complex relationship between two divergent concepts in counseling. *Journal of Counseling Psychology, 29*, 240–245.

Perls, F. (1969). *Gestalt therapy verbatim.* Lafayette, CA: Real People Press.

Pine, F. (1990). *Drive, ego, object, and self: A synthesis for clinical work.* New York: Basic Books.

Racker, H. (1957). The meanings and uses of countertransference. *Psychoanalytic Quarterly, 26*, 303–357.

Racker, H. (1968). *Transference and countertransference.* New York: International Universities Press.

Reich, A. (1951). On countertransference. *International Journal of Psychoanalysis, 32*, 25–31.

Reich, A. (1960). Further remarks on countertransference. *International Journal of Psychoanalysis, 41*, 389–395.

Reich, W. (1933). *Character analysis.* New York: Orgone Institute Press.

Reinhart, M. (1989). *Chiron and the healing journey.* New York: Penguin.

Remen, N., May, R., Young, D., & Berland, W. (1985). The wounded healer. *Saybrook Review, 5*, 84–93.

Renik, O. (1993). Analytic interaction: Conceptualizing technique in light of the analyst's irreducible subjectivity. *Psychoanalytic Quarterly, 62*, 466–495.

Renik, O. (1999). Discussion of Roy Shafer's (1999) article. *Psychoanalytic Psychology, 16*, 514–521.

Robbins, S. B., & Jolkovski, M. P. (1987). Managing countertransference feelings: An interactional model using awareness of feeling and theoretical framework. *Journal of Counseling Psychology, 34*, 276–282.

Robertiello, R. C., & Schoenewolf, G. (1987). *101 common therapeutic blunders: Countertransference and counterresistance in psychotherapy.* Northvale, NJ: Jason Aronson.

Rogers, C. R. (1951). *Client-centered therapy.* Cambridge, MA: Riverside Press.

Rogers, C. R. (1957). The necessary and sufficient conditions of therapeutic personality change. *Journal of Consulting Psychology, 21*, 95–103.

Rogers, C. R. (1975). Empathic: An unappreciated way of being. *The Counseling Psychologist, 5*, 2–10.
Rogers, C. R. (1989). Person-centered therapy. In R. Corsini & D. Wedding (Eds.), *Current psychotherapies* (4th ed., pp. 155–194). Itasca, IL: Peacock.
Rogers, C. R. (2000). Interview with Carl Rogers on the use of self in therapy. In M. Baldwin (Ed.), *The use of self in therapy* (pp. 29–38). Binghamton, NY: Haworth.
Rosenberger, E. W., & Hayes, J. A. (2002). Origins, consequences, and management of countertransference: A case study. *Journal of Counseling Psychology, 49*, 221–232.
Rudd, M. D., & Joiner, T. (1997). Countertransference and the therapeutic relationship: A cognitive perspective. *Journal of Cognitive Psychotherapy, 11*, 231–250.
Rudd, M. D., Joiner, T. E., & Rajab, M. H. (1995). Help negation after acute suicidal crisis. *Journal of Consulting and Clinical Psychology, 63*, 499–503.
Scogin, F. R. (2003). The status of self-administered treatments. *Journal of Clinical Psychology, 59*, 247–249.
Sharkin, B., & Gelso, C. J. (1993). The influence of counselor-trainee anger proneness on reactions to an angry client. *Journal of Counseling and Development, 71*, 483–487.
Simon, J. C. (1988). Criteria for therapist self-disclosure. *American Journal of Psychotherapy, 42*, 404–414.
Singer, B. A., & Luborsky, L. (1977). Countertransference: The status of clinical versus quantitative research. In A. S. Gurman & A. M. Razin (Eds.), *Effective psychotherapy: Handbook of research* (pp. 433–451). New York: Pergamon.
Singer, J. L., Sincoff, J. B., & Kolligan, J., Jr. (1989). Countertransference and cognition: Studying the psychotherapist's distortions as consequences of normal information processing. *Psychotherapy, 26*, 344–355.
Slakter, E. (Ed.). (1987). *Countertransference.* Northvale, NJ: Jason Aronson.
Snodgrass, M. E. (1994). *Voyages in classical mythology.* Santa Barbara: ABC-CLIO.
Spillius, E. B. (1992). Clinical experience of projective identification: In R. Anderson (Ed.), Clinical lectures on Klein and Bion (pp. 59–73). London: Tavistock.
Stern, A. (1923). On the counter-transference in psychoanalysis. *Psychoanalytic Review, 11*, 166–174.
Stolorow, R. D. (1991). The intersubjective context of intrapsychic experience: A decade of psychoanalytic inquiry. *Psychoanalytic Inquiry, 11*, 171–184.
Stolorow, R. D., Brandchaft, B., & Atwood, G. (1987). *Psychoanalytic treatment: An Intersubjective approach.* Hillsdale, NJ: Analytic Press.
Strupp, H. H. (1958). The psychotherapist's contribution to the treatment process. *Behavioral Science, 3*, 14–67.
Sullivan, H. S. (1954). *The psychiatric interview.* New York: Norton.
Tageson, C. W. (1982). *Humanistic psychology: A synthesis.* Homewood, IL: Dorsey Press.
Tauber, E. (1954). Exploring the therapeutic use of countertransference data. *Psychiatry, 17*, 331–336.
Thompson, C. (1956). The role of the analyst's personality in therapy. *American Journal of Psychotherapy, 10*, 347–359.
Trop, J. L., & Stolorow, R. D. (1997). Therapeutic empathy: An intersubjective perspective. In A. C. Bohart & L. S. Greenberg (Eds.), *Empathy reconsidered: New directions in psychotherapy* (pp. 279–291). Washington, DC: American Psychological Association.
Van Wagoner, S. L., Gelso, C. J., Hayes, J. A., & Diemer, R. A. (1991). Countertransference and the reputedly excellent therapist. *Psychotherapy, 28*, 411–421.
Wampold, B. E. (2001). *The great psychotherapy debate.* Mahwah, NJ: Lawrence Erlbaum Associates.
Weinshel, E., & Renik, O. (1991). The past ten years: Psychoanalysis in the United States, 1980–1990. *Psychoanalytic Inquiry, 11*, 13–29.

Wells, T. L. (1994). Therapist self-disclosure: Its effects on clients and the treatment relationship. *Smith College Studies in Social Work, 65,* 23–41.

Westen, D., Novotny, C. M., & Thompson-Brenner, H. (2004). The empirical status of empirically supported psychotherapies: Assumptions, findings, and reporting in controlled clinical trials. *Psychological Bulletin, 130,* 631–663.

Whan, M. (1987). Chiron's wound: Some reflections on the wounded healer. In N. Schwartz-Salant & M. Stein (Eds.), *Archetypal processes in psychotherapy* (pp. 197–208). Wilmette, IL: Chiron Publications.

White, W. L. (2000). The history of recovered people as wounded healers. *Alcoholism Treatment Quarterly, 18,* 1–25.

Widmer, M. A. (1995). Case histories in therapeutic recreation: The emergence of ethical issues. *Therapeutic Recreational Journal, 29,* 265–269.

Wilkinson, S. M., & Gabbard, G. O. (1993). Therapeutic self-disclosure with borderline patients. *Journal of Psychotherapy Practice and Research, 2,* 282–295.

Williams, E. N., & Fauth, J. (2005). A psychotherapy process study of therapist in-session self-awareness. *Psychotherapy Research, 15,* 374–381.

Williams, E. N., Hurley, K., O'Brien, K., & DeGregorio, A. (2003). Development and validation of the Self-awareness and Management Strategies Scales for therapists. *Psychotherapy, 40,* 278–288.

Williams, E. N., Judge, A. B., Hill, C. E., & Hoffman, M. A. (1997). Experiences of novice therapists in prepracticum: Trainees', clients', and supervisors' perceptions of therapists' personal reactions and management strategies. *Journal of Counseling Psychology, 44,* 390–399.

Williams, E. N., Polster, D., Grizzard, M. B., Rockenbaugh, J., & Judge, A. B. (2003). What happens when therapist feel bored or anxious? A qualitative study of distracting self-awareness and therapists' management strategies. *Journal of Contemporary Psychotherapy, 33,* 5–18.

Winnicott, D. W. (1949). Hate in the countertransference. *International Journal of Psychoanalysis, 30,* 69–75.

Wolgien, C. S., & Coady, N. F. (1997). Good therapists' beliefs about the development of their helping ability: The wounded healer paradigm revisited. *The Clinical Supervisor, 15,* 19–35.

Yalom, I. (2002). *The gift of therapy: An open letter to a new generation of therapists and their patients.* New York: HarperCollins.

Yontef, G. M. (1993). *Awareness, dialogue, and process: Essays in gestalt therapy.* Highland, NJ: The Gestalt Journal Press.

Yulis, S., & Kiesler, D. J. (1968). Countertransference response as a function of therapist anxiety and content of patient talk. *Journal of Consulting and Clinical Psychology, 32,* 413–419.

About the Authors

Charles J. Gelso received his doctorate in psychology from Ohio State University in 1970. His primary research and clinical interests throughout his career have focused on the therapeutic relationship in psychotherapy. Within this context, he has studied and written extensively about the working alliance, transference and countertransference, and what may be termed the real relationship in psychotherapy. Dr. Gelso has authored five books and numerous journal articles and chapters, and he have been given many awards during his career. He has been Associate Editor and Editor of the *Journal of Counseling Psychology*, and currently is Editor of *Psychotherapy: Theory, Research, Practice, and Training*. He has also been involved in the practice of individual psychotherapy throughout his career.

Jeffrey A. Hayes is Professor of Counseling Psychology at Penn State University, where he has taught since 1993. He has held positions as Associate Editor of *Psychotherapy Research*, President of the North American Society for Psychotherapy Research, and Chair of the Education and Training Committee for the American Psychological Association's Division of Psychotherapy. Dr. Hayes has received early career awards for his scholarship from the Society for Psychotherapy Research and the American Psychological Association's Division of Psychotherapy. Dr. Hayes' primary professional interests are in the areas of countertransference, psychotherapy process, and the integration of spirituality and psychology. He maintains a private psychotherapy practice in State College, Pennsylvania.

Author Index

J

K

L

M

N

O

P

Subject Index

I

L

M

R

U

V

W